EX LIBRIS

CREATING CONTRAST

with

DARK PLANTS

This book is dedicated to

'A Ray of Light in a Heart of Darkness'

CREATING CONTRAST

with

DARK PLANTS

Freya Martin

GUILD OF MASTER CRAFTSMAN PUBLICATIONS

First published 2000 by
Guild of Master Craftsman Publications Ltd
166 High Street, Lewes, East Sussex BN7 1XU

© in the Work GMC Publications Ltd
Text © Freya Martin 2000

Illustrations by Liz Pepperell
Photographic credits, including cover shots, page 142

ISBN 1 86108 164 2

Cover and book designed by Fran Rawlinson
Typefaces: Lithos and Sabon

Colour origination by Viscan Graphics (Singapore)

Printed and bound by Kyodo Printing (Singapore) under
the supervision of MRM Graphics, Winslow, Buckinghamshire, UK

CONTENTS

NOTES

DIMENSIONS OF PLANTS

Dimensions are given in metric, with imperial equivalents in brackets. Inevitably these are approximate, depending on geographical location and conditions in which any plant is grown, and they should be treated as a rough guideline only.

PHOTOGRAPHS OF PLANTS

Every effort has been made to select photographs which represent the true colours of the plants included in this book. However, variables such as light conditions, photographic film and processing, age and natural variations of stock, may make some plants appear to be lighter in colour than when seen with the naked eye.

THE NAMING OF PLANTS

Wherever possible, the plant names that appear in this book have been checked against *Plant Finder 1999–2000,* The Royal Horticultural Society's authoritative publication. This lists plant names approved by the Society's Advisory Panel on Nomenclature and Taxonomy, which was set up to establish the agreed list of plant names now held on the RHS database. However, naming plants is a very complex task: nurseries and users of *Plant Finder* are continually proposing name changes and, in addition, reclassifications are being made due to the increasing sophistication of genetically based research. The list is therefore updated constantly and, while efforts have been made to include previous names, in the format 'new name' syn. 'previous name', some of the species listed in this book do not feature in *Plant Finder*.

Plants in the Choosing Dark Plants section (pp. 8–107) are listed alphabetically under their Latin names, followed in brackets by their common (i.e. colloquial, everyday) name, where known. To make it easy to look up a particular plant, both Latin and common names are listed in the index and cross-referenced.

Referring to plants by their Latin name may seem confusing, but in fact it is more accurate than using common names, which can vary from country to country or even from one local region to another.

The system for classifying plants by Latin name was originally devised by Carl von Linné – a Swedish botanist – in the eighteenth century. This system was accepted internationally and, although it has been modified over the years, it is now the acknowledged form of nomenclature within the horticultural world.

Under the Linnaeus system (named after Carl von Linné), plants are divided into groups, according to common characteristics. All plants have a double Latin name, the first being the name of the genus or wider grouping, and the second denoting the particular species within that genus; these enable us to identify a precise plant with accuracy.

Sometimes, when referring generally to a group of plants, the genus name is used on its own, e.g. 'geranium'. However, a genus may contain up to several hundred species of related plants, each exhibiting slight variations in flower and fruit. The plants within such a genus therefore need to be more precisely described by adding the species name, e.g. *Geranium pyrenaicum.*

In addition, further names are frequently added to describe the more subtle differences in colour and size of individual plants, or groups of similar plants (subspecies), within a species. These differences may be naturally occurring and are then termed 'varieties' (indicated, though not always, by 'var.', e.g. *Geranium phaeum* var. *variegatum*). They may, alternatively, be the result of breeding programmes and are then termed 'cultivars' (indicated by a name in single quotes, e.g. *Geranium phaeum* 'Samobor'). Hybrids occur naturally and artificially from the cross-breeding of parent plants from within or between genera (indicated by 'x', e.g. *Geranium* x *oxonianum).*

AUTHOR'S NOTE ON CATEGORIES

I have divided the plants into three principal 'dark' categories: 'Flowers'; 'Foliage'; and 'Trees, Shrubs and Grasses'. I could have categorized them by size, season or site, which are crucial factors for any gardener, but have put these details in the 'Grow How' box accompanying each plant entry.

Flowers – the largest dark category – are subdivided into three sections: 'Annuals, Biennials and Tender Perennials'; 'Bulbs, Corms, Rhizomes and Tubers'; and 'Hardy Perennials'.

Foliage plants have their own section as they are a vital part of any border, adding substance and structure. They are subdivided into 'Annuals, Biennials and Tender Perennials' (including succulents); and 'Hardy Perennials'.

'Trees, Shrubs and Grasses', which are listed alphabetically, have their own section too, because of their size, and also because of their dark foliage, dark flowers or dark stem colouring.

I chose the above section divisions because my main aim was to categorize plants according to their ability to survive in a temperate climate – my own natural habitat. However, I also wanted to keep all the plants in the 'Bulbs, Corms, Rhizomes and Tubers' section together, because of their botanical attributes. You will therefore see both tender and hardy perennials in this section.

In such cases, and indeed others in the plant directory, I have, on the basis of a temperate climate, indicated which plants are suitable only for indoors or temporary outdoor exposure, as well as those which are likely to be tender, or half-hardy to hardy, or semi-evergreen to evergreen outdoors. Additionally, the native origins of most of the plants are also listed, as an extra guide to whether they will tolerate the conditions of your particular garden.

However, a couple of plants have escaped from the 'Bulbs, Corms, Rhizomes and Tubers' section. A rhizomatous perennial, the aquilegia, is in the 'Hardy Perennials' section because I can only think of it as a hardy perennial cottage garden favourite, and so invoke author's prerogative! Likewise, only a couple of the foliage plants are rhizomatous or tuberous, and would have been lonely in their own section, so they are included under 'Hardy' or 'Tender Perennials', as appropriate.

A last note: if you cannot find a favourite plant, and want to check if it comes in a dark shade, try the index – but please take time to discover other dark plants as well.

A POTTED INTRODUCTION

The aim of this book is simple – it is to introduce the colour-conscious gardener to plants with black, or nearly black, flowers and foliage.

The compilation of a selection of dark plants of all sizes and for all situations hasn't been without its problems. It would have been a lot easier (and a lot less original) to have compiled a book on white plants. It would also have been a much heavier tome.

Black or nearly black plants are not so easy to track down, and many's the time I have been disappointed to find my 'Black Knight' (or 'Night') in shining armour has turned out to be bright red!

Truly black plants are rare creatures, but many other plants are dark-coloured and therefore certainly merit inclusion in this book when they are often ignored in others. But to include or exclude? The decision has been somewhat subjective, as it can't be based on the simple biological fact of a black pigment – it doesn't exist. Moreover, many nearly black plants appear darker when they are positioned in bright sunlight. This isn't just a 'trick of the light', but a chemical reaction to the sun's rays which is particularly noticeable on dark foliage. The black and nearly black plants in this collection achieve their look from underlying pigments of purple (primarily), red and blue, and even green, which is often more apparent as flowers fade and die. Hence, you'll find many of the plants described as black-red, purple-black, etc. These perhaps are poor descriptions, but the photographs illustrate the precise nature of their colour and beauty more

Tulipa 'Black Swan'

Viola 'Molly Sanderson'

effectively than I am able to do in prose.

Of course, a lot of black and nearly black plants are not natural, but the result of slow and laborious (but passionate) breeding programmes. The greatest successes have been in the hellebores, irises, peonies and violas, largely because of the original genetic make-up that Nature has 'given' us to play with.

While plant breeders have their practical problems when creating the darkest-coloured cultivars of particular plants, dark plants generally present me with another problem. Why, when there are so many beautiful dark plants, have they made so little impact on the gardening scene?

When I was photographing black hellebores at Ashwood Nursery, in the West Midlands, a gardener commented that they were just downright ugly, and black plants definitely wouldn't find a place in his garden. His companion was of the opposite view, regarding dark blooms as luxuriously exotic. Why do they engender such a diverse reaction?

The decision to use or not to use dark plants in our gardens is, I think, more than just a question of taste. While we are attracted to the ethereal, ghostly quality of the all-white garden, at the same time we exhibit a degree of superstitious aversion to black flowers because of the morbid associations we make.

The colour black is certainly linked to the most negative area of our lives, death. But this is unfair. Black is not the only colour associated with death: the Chinese and the Sri

Lankans, for instance, use white for funereal garb. Lord Tennyson's Lady of Shallott floats dying, down the stream after 'the mirror crack'd', '... robed in snowy white/That loosely flew to left and right' (Part IV).

In Western culture, the use of both white and black (the former usually for the death of the young and/or virtuous) goes back to Ancient Greece. But other colours have also been socially acceptable for mourning, including red: a picture of the funeral of the French King Charles VI in 1422 shows members of the *Parlement* of Paris resplendent in red and ermine robes. In any case, during the Middle Ages and the Elizabethan and Jacobean periods, black-dyed cloth was of the very highest quality and price and reserved for the aristocracy, rather like the imperial purple before. But by Victorian times black had become the dominant colour in their complicated mourning dress code. Black and its association with death has been indelibly printed on our psyche by imagery which ranges from the writings of Edgar Allan Poe to the pictures of a mourning Queen Victoria.

The ritual surrounding the death of royalty has always been a little ambivalent however, because it is so closely linked to the celebration of a coronation: 'The king is dead. Long live the king.' In Ghana still, at the coronation of an Ashanti king, his close retinue wear black and carry black, red and gold coloured parasols.

But let's move away from clothes to what this book is about, flowers. In the seventeenth-century elegy by Milton of 'Lycidas', both black and white flowers are used together: pansies streaked with jet and white carnations are strewn upon his hearse. The real use of white flowers in relation to funerals is documented from more ancient times. Remains of white Madonna lilies have been found in the tomb of the Tutankhamun, alongside the physical remains of wreaths which included red poppies, blue cornflowers and white waterlilies. But it was in fact the perfume not the flowers of white lilies which was found. Though this particular example may be partially discounted, nevertheless the white lily was used, and 'commonly grown on graves because it lasts well', so said the first-century Roman natural historian Pliny the Elder. It is therefore curious to me why so many modern brides like to be seen with white lilies in their hand, but maybe that is a subconscious comment on the state of matrimony in the modern world!

A study of the symbolic value of the white lily would fill a treatise: from its religious connotations in the Pre-Raphaelite painting *Ecce Ancilla Domini!* by Dante Gabriel Rossetti, to its use as a Shakespearean literary metaphor at both ends of the morality scale.

Ocimum basilicum 'Purple Ruffles'

White flowers continue to be used for funerals: from the white calico roses on graves in Mexico, to the white chrysanthemums at public eulogies in Japan.

The white calico roses have been made famous in the paintings by Georgia O'Keeffe, in which she positioned them next to the sand-blasted bones of animals in the New Mexico desert in the late 1920s. This imagery marks, in simplistic terms, a transition to the barren for O'Keeffe, both in terms of life and painting, which earlier in the decade had seen her produce large canvases showing in close-up the vitality of colourful, living, sexual flowers. Several black-coloured flowers were her subjects: the hollyhock, iris, jack-in-the-pulpit, pansy and petunia.

One flower that doesn't feature in her work is the tulip, which in historical and literary terms is the most famous, or infamous, of flowers, and was immortalized in *The Black Tulip* by Alexandre Dumas published in 1850. The meaning of the tulip is – and it would seem always has been – love, whether in fables from the land of its origin, Turkey, or in the language of flowers of the Victorian period,

when types of love were associated with different coloured tulips. But in Dumas, the meaning of love is subverted by the black tulip which becomes a double-edged sword: it is a metaphor for good triumphing over the evils of avarice, obsession and fatality, but to which weaker spirits can also succumb when faced with the black tulip's unique and priceless, yet pure, beauty.

The protagonist Cornelius van Baerle's efforts to grow a truly black tulip, and the attendant misery, were based on very real events in the sixteenth century in mainland Europe, particularly Holland (the country which is now synonymous with the tulip), when the craze for novel tulips bankrupted many a man and brought about a virtual collapse of the entire economy. Today, we do have a small selection of black tulips to enjoy, but even though they are beautiful plants, I doubt if they arouse quite the same passions.

Dark flowers also feature in the disturbing, yet faintly ridiculous, novel *Against Nature* by J. K. Huysmans. The principal character, Des Esseintes (thought to be based on the author himself) will go to any lengths to live a life of hedonistic artifice, and this includes (among the less outrageous examples) surrounding himself with exotic flowers which must be at once real, yet appear inanimate and artificial. Included within his collection is the amorphophallus (*Dracunculus vulgaris*), which features in one of his drug-induced nightmares, and the description of which, suffice it to say, relates to death and sex. It is joined, alongside flesh-coloured plants, by other dark plants such as black-leaved begonias and crotons.

But while black plants may occasionally be used for dark metaphor, this is by no means exclusive. Neither is there a history of dark-coloured plants being used for dark deeds.

The nearest case may be that of the black hellebore, and while that plant may feature in the Garden of Proserpina alongside the opium

Tulipa 'Black Beauty'

poppy in Spenser's *Faerie Queene*, the name, according to Pliny the Elder, refers not to the colour of the flower but of the root. He gives many examples of the medical, but dangerous and deadly, uses to which this plant (and many, many others) could be put, but it is clear from his tract that the white hellebore was the more lethal of the two.

On the one hand the hellebore was used by the ancient Gauls as a poison for their arrow tips, and on the other collected (after the gatherer had fortified himself against its powers with a good dose of garlic and wine) to use in elaborate ritual to ward off ill omen.

Ancient cultures have consistently had an ambiguous relationship with such powerful plants, as they were seen as cure-alls but they could also easily kill.

Ambiguity is also the key to our relationship with the colour black. It is at one and the same time the colour of safety and of danger; of the establishment and conformity, and the individual and rebellion.

Whether you want your garden to wear the colour black as a sign of rebellion against the pastel scenery, or as a sign of Byronic romanticism or avant-garde chic, read on to see the many choices that are available.

Cimifuga simplex 'Brunette'

The following section presents a selection of dark plants divided into flowering and foliage groups, which are further subdivided into annuals, biennials and tender perennials; hardy perennials; flowering bulbs, corms, rhizomes and tubers; and a selection of trees, shrubs and grasses. The plants are of all sizes, from 6cm–30m (2½in–90ft), and for all situations, whether outdoors or in.

CHOOSING
DARK
PLANTS

FLOWERS

ANNUALS, BIENNIALS AND TENDER PERENNIALS

ALCEA ROSEA SYN. *ALTHAEA ROSEA* (HOLLYHOCK)

The majestic hollyhock has been a popular garden feature, not just in this country but also in Persia, where it features in art dating back to the fifteenth century. But, like a lot of traditional cottage garden plants, the hollyhock originally earned its place for more than its looks. The cottage garden was as much a source for cooking and folk medicine as beauty, although today the latter is now the determining factor. In the case of the hollyhock, its active chemical ingredients were used against cystitis and stomachaches, and are now to be found as derivatives in modern medicines.

A Dark Selection

A. 'Black Beauty'
Black fading out slightly to maroon edges.

A. 'Arabian Nights'
Deep red-black wet look with a fuschia-red corona around a creamy-white centre.

A. 'Double Arabian Nights'
Similar in shading to its single-flowered cousin.

Black-coloured blooms can also be found in mixed selections such as 'East Coast (east of England that is) Hybrids' for single flowers and 'Chater's Double Group'.

Strictly speaking, the hollyhock is a hardy perennial which can be treated as an annual, but it is in fact best treated as a

Alcea rosea 'Nigra', another dark cultivar

GROW HOW

Size: 150–180cm (5–6ft).

Season: July–August.

Site: Drained soil. Sheltered position. Full sun.

Propagation: Seed.

Alcea rosea 'Chater's Double Group'

biennial. The extra effort to grow it as a biennial will be rewarded with better-looking stronger blooms and will also reduce the risk of rust, to which the hollyhock can be prone.

Prepare alternate cycles of sowing to ensure biennial blooms every year, but uproot those biennials which have flowered. If you prefer to leave the plants *in situ*, be sure to cut them right down and get rid of the debris; this will reduce the chance of rust and other diseases spreading from old to new growth. As in all cases of rust infection, any plant matter affected should be removed and burned.

The hollyhock is easy to grow, and can germinate in as little as two weeks in the right conditions. Like many cottage plants it is excellent at self-propagating, and this feature is essential for creating an authentic cottage garden feel. But, if you don't like Nature to take its course, remove those plants you don't want – but remember that it's better to discard them completely than try to relocate them, as they resent being moved. Alternatively, you can collect the seed and sow it yourself.

For biennial planting, sow previously collected seed in the warm summer months. This will allow the plants to become established over a longer period, and they will then flower well the following summer.

If you really can't wait, treat it as an annual plant and, during January–February, sprinkle the seed into pots. If you leave the pots uncovered in a warm place or propagator, at a temperature of at least 16°C (60°F), you can expect germination to occur in one to three months. Once the plants have reached a suitable size and all chance of a cold spell and frost has passed, harden them off and plant out. Alternatively you can sow seeds outdoors in position during May–June for flowers the same year.

CENTAUREA CYNANUS (CORNFLOWER)

The cornflower is excellent for cut flowers and 'Black Ball', which is one of the tall varieties of cornflower, is well suited to this purpose and can create more unusual colour mixes.

Centaurea 'Black Ball'

GROW HOW

Size: 75cm (29½in)

Season: June – September.

Site: Any soil. Full sun.

Propagation: Seed.

For an abundance of flowers, sow in the flowering position in early spring in tilthed soil and cover with approximately 5mm (¼in) of compost. Alternatively sow in late summer to early autumn for plants the following year.

DIANTHUS (CARNATION & SWEET WILLIAM)

Dianthus barbatus

Dianthus barbatus (sweet william) and *D. caryophyllus* (carnation) are combined under this one heading.

Carnation is a word that has evolved from the Latin through to its current form, which itself dates back to the Elizabethan period. The carnation was one of a number of flowers used in garlands – in Latin, *corona(e)* – hence coronation, to cornation, to carnation. Another Elizabethan name for this flower was gillyflower, which is a corruption of the Latin word for clove. Cloves were an expensive imported commodity, so carnation petals were often substituted to flavour wine. The carnation was also used as a sign of betrothal, and even today is probably still the most popular 'buttonhole' at weddings.

A Dark Selection

D. b. 'Charcoal'
60cm (23½in). Purple-grey flowers tinged with bright red for an unusual effect.

D. b. 'Sooty'
30cm (12in). An old variety, with red-black shading on the good-sized flowerheads; these surmount reddish stems and are surrounded by charcoal-tinged leaves, which can remain evergreen in mild climates.

D. c. Black and White Minstrels Group
30cm(12in). An unfortunate non-PC name for such a pretty flower, red-black edged with white, with a fragrant perfume.

D. c. 'Chianti'
30cm (12in). A double bloom, richly tinged with burgundy.

D. c. 'King of the Blacks'
60cm (23½in). The darkest?

D. c. 'Velvet 'n' Lace'
30cm (12in). A double bloom in deep purple-black with more white edging than Black and White Minstrels.

The dianthus is a fairly drought-tolerant plant, and though a perennial is pretty much always treated as an annual or biennial. Being a perennial, it can be propagated by division in the spring or autumn, as well as by seed.

GROW HOW

Size: Various.

Season: June–September.

Site: Well-drained, neutral to alkaline soil. Full sun.

Propagation: Division/Seed.

Sow seed in the spring to early summer in pots barely covered with compost; it will then flower the following year. Depending on your garden's location and the severity of winter conditions, plant out the young plants in either the autumn or following spring.

Dianthus barbatus Nigricans – an alternative choice

ERYSIMUM (WALLFLOWER)

An older English common name for erysimum is heart's ease, but this name is more often applied to the viola, which was used in love potions in that connection. Wallflowers were once thought to increase the yield of apple trees if planted at their bases. These days, this short-lived perennial is often used as an annual in municipal mixed bedding schemes.

GROW HOW

Size: 30–45cm (12–18in)

Season: April–June.

Site: Well-drained yet moist, neutral to alkaline soil. Full sun.

Propagation: Cuttings/Seed.

You can take softwood cuttings in the summer, but seed is readily available. Seed should be sown in pots in late spring to early summer; you can then move the plants outside to their flowering position in the autumn, and they will produce early flowers the following year. Erysimum will do well in a wide range of soil conditions, in fact it does better in terms of flowers on poor quality soil.

Erysimum 'Bowles Mauve'

HELIANTHUS (SUNFLOWER)

The sunflower is a popular modern motif, and an ideal plant for young children developing their 'green fingers', as its fast growing-cycle produces tall plants in a short time.

A Dark Selection

H. Chianti'
Red-black centre fading out to deep red petals.

H. 'Prado Red'
Red-black with a touch or burnt umber like a corona of light. This cultivar is better for hayfever sufferers as it produces hardly any pollen.

H. 'Velvet Queen'
Deep red-black with a very dark centre, making this perhaps the darkest available.

Helianthus 'Prado Red'

GROW HOW

Size: 120–150cm (4–5ft)

Season: Summer.

Site: Drained, rich soil. Full sun.

Propagation: Seed.

The sunflower is very quick and easy to grow, taking as little as one week to germinate and reaching maturity in two months in ideal conditions. Growing so fast, it often requires staking. It thrives in manure-enriched soil, but does well else-where, if there is plenty of warm sunshine.

Sow seed outside in April, either in individual pots for planting out later, or in in their final position – in a border or large-sized container – thinning out as necessary. Only use pots for dwarf varieties, rather than the full-sized such as 'Velvet Queen' which, if containerised, will not reach their full height. Because they grow so quickly, it is important that they receive regular feed and water, especially if they are pot-grown. Also keep an eye out for slugs and snails during the early stages of growth.

You can acheive an impressive display, if you allow the plant to grow naturally, so that it produces several short-stemmed flowers off the central main stem; but, if you prefer larger flowers on longer stems, pinch out some of the side buds.

The seeds are attractive to birds and humans alike. When the petals start to fade, collect the numerous seeds for next year's plants and for hungry birds in winter.

KENNEDIA NIGRICANS (BLACK BEAN FLOWER, BLACK CORAL PEA)

This vigorous climber from Australia has brown/purple-black flowers with golden-yellow markings, which hang down in small racemes. It is a suitable plant for a cool greenhouse or conservatory, and is a half-hardy to hardy perennial depending on your situation.

Unlike most other plants, the seeds of *K. nigricans* literally get you into hot water: you don't put the seeds in the fridge, but pour boiling water over them and then soak them in tepid water overnight to encourage germination. As long as the temperature is around 20°C (68°F) when the seeds are planted, germination should occur within three months.

You could also propagate by taking semi-ripe cuttings from the plant in summer.

Prune after flowering, and do not water during the winter months.

Kennedia nigricans

GROW HOW

Size: Up to 6m (18ft)

Season: Late spring to summer.

Site: Sandy, well-drained soil. Full sun.

Propagation: Cuttings/Seed.

LARDIZABALA BITERNATA (ZABALA FRUIT)

From Chile, where its fruit is widely eaten, this fairly vigorous climber has brown-black drooping flowers. To be on the safe side, treat it as a tender perennial; it is best to plant it in a warm, protected spot or in a cool greenhouse/conservatory, although it can be hardy to −10°C (12°F).

Another dark climber from the same family of Lardizabalaceae is the akebia. Either *A. quinata* (chocolate vine) or *A. trifoliata* (syn. *A. lobata*) provide a slightly more hardy alternative; these can be semi-evergreen in mild locations, but should be lightly cut back in autumn and protected from frosts.

GROW HOW

Size: Up to 3m (9ft).

Season: Summer.

Site: Well-drained, yet humus-rich soil. Full sun to partial shade.

Propagation: Cuttings/Seed.

Akebia quinata

New plants can be grow from seed sown in spring, or from stem cuttings taken in late summer to early autumn.

NEMOPHILA

A native of California, nemophila, with its floriferous spreading habit, is a good plant for both hanging baskets and edging in other containers, or as loosely structured groundcover.

A Dark Selection

N. insignis (formerly *N. menziesii*) 'Pennie (Penny) Black'
Purple-black flowers just under 25mm (1in) across, enhanced with a white underside and white edging.

N. discoidalis 'Total Eclipse'
So-called perhaps because of the starburst-like centre and the corona of white encircling the purple-black (but more bronzed than 'Pennie Black') petals.

Nemophila is very easy to grow from seed, if sown in the flowering position between March and May, on well-drained raked soil, and barely covered. Alternatively, it can be sown in autumn into propagators for planting out in spring; however, since it only takes about two weeks to germinate, this hardly seems worth the bother.

Nemophila insignis 'Penny Black'

GROW HOW

Size: 10–15cm (4–6in) tall x 30–40cm (12–16in) spread.

Season: June–September.

Site: Moist soil. Full sun to partial shade.

Propagation: Seed.

PAPAVER SOMNIFERUM (OPIUM POPPY)

The common name, opium poppy, is in fact a misnomer when this poppy is grown in temperate climes. The seeds, whether dusted on freshly baked bread or ground up for oil, provide a high only in the sense of calories.

A Dark Selection

P. somniferum
Single black exotic blooms about 10cm (4in) in diameter with white filaments inside, creating attractive seedheads.

P. somniferum paeoniflorum 'Black Beauty'
Purple-black, very double bloom which, as the name says, belongs to the 'Peony-flowered Series'.

P. somniferum paeoniflorum 'Black Paeony'
Double blooms in darkest maroon black.

A dark-coloured double is also available from the mixed selection 'Summer Fruits' which consists mainly of pink shades, but which also includes a very deep maroon 'Blackberry' bloom. If you aren't keen on the large size of the *Papaver somniferum*

GROW HOW

Size: 90–120cm (3–4ft).

Season: July–September.

Site: Drained soil. Full sun.

Propagation: Seed.

Papaver somniferum 'Guinness'

Papaver somniferum

You can sow seeds for this plant at almost any time between spring and early summer, but they are best sown in autumn. When freshly collected the seed is abundant and the decorative blue seedheads are a feature in their own right. The poppy can be a prolific self-seeder and, if you allow autumnal winds to disperse the seed, you may be surprised (or annoyed) at where they establish themselves.

The seed is fine, and does best when sown in finely raked soil and lightly covered. In a sunny, well-drained site the seeds will begin to germinate when temperatures reach around 16°C (60°F) and should then take three to four weeks to produce seedlings. Thin the seedlings out earlier, rather than later, to encourage strong growth.

Alternatively sow in pots and plant out well before the young plants become pot bound, as moving them late in their development would cause stress and affect the plants ability to produce good quality flowers.

there are some purple-bronze shades of *Eschscholzia californica* (California poppy) which have a rather more delicate appearance, but unfortunately these are also more susceptible to attack by slugs.

When fully grown the poppy may need some support or companion planting, as it has a tendency to flop outwards, and this leaves a bare centre.

PELARGONIUM

Pelargoniums are the familiar bedding plants of parks and gardens, and are particularly suited to container-growing. Many people still refer to them as 'geraniums', because they were originally included in the geranium genus. Much confusion arose, and so in recent years the pelargoniums were separated and they now sit comfortably on their own, although of course they are still related closely to the hardy herbaceous geraniums (see page 55).

As tender perennials, they require a warm situation and, given this, they will thrive for a long time with regular deadheading.

Pelargonium 'Lord Bute'

A Dark Selection

The dark pelargoniums are predominantly of the regal type and fall into the red-black area of the colour spectrum:

P. 'Black Butterfly'

P. 'Black Velvet'
Also tinged dark purple.

P. 'Dark Venus'

P. 'Fifth Avenue'

P. 'Jungle Knight'
Slightly ruffled petals.

P. 'Lord Bute'
Also an almost cerise narrow edging.

P. 'Minstrel Boy'

P. 'Morwenna'
Fading to mahogany.

P. 'Pompeii'
Brownish red-black with white edging.

P. *sidoides*
Red-black above scented leaves.

For bi- or tricolour foliage, try the zonal pelargoniums, such as 'Turkish Delight' and 'Golden Ears'. Other cultivars of note are 'Distinction', with a black ring on a green leaf, and 'Mephistopheles' with its completely black foliage.

Seed will not come true for named varieties,

Pelargonium 'Pompeii'

GROW HOW

Size: 40 x 40cm (15¾ x 15¾in).
Season: May–October.
Site: Well-drained soil. Full sun.
Propagation: Cuttings/Seed.

but, should you decide to give it a go anyway, pre-chill the seed and sow it in early spring; it will require a minimum of 21°C (70°F) to germinate.

Softwood cuttings can be taken any time between spring and autumn, and should be shaded from the light for about two weeks while roots are established. Tip cuttings taken just above a leaf node should be protected in the same way. In fact, whatever the pelargonium's age, it should not be exposed to harsh sunlight. Water

young plants regularly (regals are thirstier than most), and feed (particularly with potassium) and pinch out to produce the best blooms.

Although some pelargonium varieties are quite hardy for what are often only thought of as disposable summer bedding, the regal's blooms are quite easily marked and damaged by summer showers. If you are treating them as tender perennials, they will need to be overwintered in warm conditions above 10°C (50°F).

Keep inside until late May. Before putting out, cut them back quite radically to around two-thirds of their previous season's growth, pruning each stem to just above a leaf node to reduce die-back; at the same time, take the opportunity to improve the shape of any of your plants that have become a bit untidy.

PRIMULA GOLD LACE GROUP

This primula belongs to the polyanthus group of primula and is a cultivar from *Primula obconica*, sometimes called the German primrose (although in fact it comes from China). The Gold Lace Group has mahogany heart-shaped petals with a distinctive, contrasting golden eye and edging. The petals are certainly attractive, but those with sensitive skin should beware the leaves, which can cause a painful allergic reaction.

The primula genus is generally perennial (see *Primula auricula*, on page 63), but *P. obconica* is treated as annual, hence its inclusion here.

Keep plants fed and moist at all times, but particularly just before and during flowering, and especially if pot grown.

For next year's plants, it is best to sow the seed as soon as it is available, but seed can be sown up to about July. Barely cover the seed with compost and place it in a propagator, or cover with polythene, to keep the moisture in. Germination requires a temperature of at least 16°C (61°F).

Keep out of the light until the shoots appear, and keep the young plants shaded over the summer. Re-pot as necessary.

GROW HOW

Size: 20–30cm (8–12in).

Season: December–May.

Site: Well-drained to gritty loam-based soil. Sheltered situation in partial to full shade.

Propagation: Seed.

Primula Gold Lace Group

This species is often grown as a pot plant for winter colour, but it can survive outdoors, provided it is planted out later during its flowering period in a warm and sheltered position, with a temperature always kept above 7°C (45°F).

SALPIGLOSSIS

This is a genus of half-hardy annuals and biennials, but usually only annuals are cultivated, either for colour in borders or as greenhouse plants.

A Dark Selection

S. 'Chocolate Pot'
30cm (12in). A mahogany centre fading out to brown-black with a tiny golden eye.

S. 'Gloomy Rival'
60–75cm (23½–29½in). A strange coloration best described as brown/grey-black.

Salpiglossis seed needs a temperature of around 18°C (64°F) to germinate, so sow under glass in late winter/early spring, and then plant out during May. It can also be sown *in situ* in April/May, when all fear of frost has passed.

To provide winter colour indoors, seed can be sown in pots in September.

Deadhead the plants regularly, to keep the flowers coming.

GROW HOW
Size: Various.
Season: July–September.
Site: Fertile soil. Full sun.
Propagation: Seed.

SCABIOSA ATROPURPUREA (SWEET SCABIOUS, PINCUSHION FLOWER)

A cottage garden classic which comes in both annual and perennial varieties, and which is believed to relieve itchy skin conditions, hence the name derived from the Latin *scabies*. But keep it in the garden rather than bring it indoors as a cut flower, as according to old English lore this will mean the Devil will visit you in the night! The atropurpurea variety is an annual which is native to South Africa. It could be a perennial for a few brief warm years if you are lucky.

A Dark Selection

S. a. 'Ace of Spades'
S. a. 'Black Widow'
S. a. 'Chile Black'

Those listed are all in various shades of purple-black florets dusted with fine white stamens.

Sow seeds in the flowering position during April–May, in tilted soil; add grit or gravel to help improve the drainage if you have particularly heavy soil, and lightly cover.

GROW HOW

Size: 60–90cm (23½in–35½in).
Season: July.
Site: Neutral to alkaline, well-drained soil. Full sun.
Propagation: Seed.

Scabiosa atropurpurea 'Ace of Spades'

TACCA CHANTRIERI (BAT FLOWER)

This plant was introduced from the Far East towards the end of the nineteenth century.

Narrowly oblong, stalked, arching leaves are 45cm (18in) or more long, and in summer it produces flower umbels with green or purplish bracts on stems up to 60cm (2ft) long. The individual green flowers turn purple, and have long pendent, maroon to purple 'tendrils' which can invoke a shudder! This is a disturbing yet mesmerizing plant which, as the common name suggests, is reminiscent of a bat because of the shape of its upright petals. It has an equally strange, anaemic cousin, *T. chantrieri* 'Alba'.

This plant is difficult to raise from seed,

GROW HOW

Size: 60–90cm (23½–35½in.

Season: Summer.

Site: Drained soil. Partial shade.

Propagation: Seed.

and it can take anything up to nine months to germinate, since it needs really warm conditions that reach at least 27°C (80°F). Because of this, although it is a clump-forming rhizomatous perennial in its natural habitat, for many of us it is only suitable as a greenhouse plant, which may be placed outdoors in the hot summer months and then overwintered indoors.

Tacca chantrieri

TROPAEOLUM (NASTURTIUM)

The dark red-brown petals and dark foliage of the dwarf cultivated *Tropaeolum* 'King Theodore' has been around since the end of the nineteenth century. Nasturtiums actually flower better in poorer quality, but well-drained, soil.

Sow seed in the flowering position in April, thinning out the seedlings as necessary. Alternatively sow them in trays a couple of months earlier in a greenhouse to bring them on sooner, remembering to harden off the young plants gradually before planting them out towards the end of April.

GROW HOW

Size: 25–30cm (10–12in).

Season: June–September.

Site: Well-drained, poor quality soil. Full sun.

Propagation: Seed.

VIOLA x WITTROCKIANA (PANSY)

The common name derives from the French, *pensée* for 'thought' as states Hamlet's *Ophelia* (Act IV, scene V). Superstitious lore says not to pick a pansy with dew on, as this will cause the death of a loved one – this may give added meaning to its inclusion in Ophelia's bouquet as she mourns the death of her father Apollonius.

Viola 'Black Beauty'

A Dark Selection

Many pansies have a centre that is more or less black, but those listed below are either totally, or predominantly, black. No doubt there are plenty more that I have not included, but see also violets, page 66, in the Hardy Perennials section.

V. 'Black Beauty'
V. 'Black Prince'
V. 'Black Star'
V. 'Bowles' Black'
V. 'King of the Blacks'
V. 'Springtime Black'

Some Bicolours

V. 'Brunig'
Very dark brown-black with a narrow edging of deep yellow.

V. 'Oberon'
Brown-black with golden picotee edging.

V. 'Rippling Waters'
A distinctive, pretty white-bordered, large-flowered blue-black pansy.

V. 'Rococo'
Dating back to the Victorian era, a range of ruffled petals in opulent shades combining with black.

GROW HOW

Size: 15–20cm (6–8in).

Season: April–September with repeat sowing between March–July.

Site: Drained soil, but pretty much anywhere. Full sun to partial shade.

Propagation: Seed.

Pansies are really easy to grow, and seed germinates in two–three weeks.

Sow under cover between December and March, or outdoors between March and July, or even later for flowers the following year. It is important that the temperature does not exceed around 10°C (50°F), as too hot conditions will prevent germination.

FLOWERS

BULBS, CORMS, RHIZOMES AND TUBERS

ARISAEMA (COBRA LILY)

A shade-loving plant painted several times by Georgia O'Keeffe. Many have been (and still are being) collected from the wild in the Far East, consequently their existence in their natural habitat is in danger. They can however be found in the specialist nursery, which propagates new stock.

A related variety, *A. triphyllum* (better known as Jack-in-the-pulpit) has also been represented in art, as a fluid bulbous glass vase by Tiffany. Several other species belonging to the family of Aroids also find themselves included in this collection of dark plants.

A Dark Selection

A. consanguineum
Striped spathes of white and dark purple-brown measuring 30–40cm (12–16in).

A. griffithi var. *pradhanii*
A very dark brown-purple spathe with a slightly wrinkled appearance, on this low-growing variety.

A. sikokianum
A brown-black partially striped spathe approximately 20cm (8in) on stems up to 30cm (12in) tall contrasts dramatically

Arisaema sikokianum

with a pure white knob-ended spadix, shaded by large almost marbled leaves.

A borderline candidate is *A. ringens*, which has a black-purple interior to its green and white striped spathe.

The arisaema likes a moist, shady site, but avoid cold and boggy conditions. Despite its exotic appearance, it is quite hardy – but protect it from frosts if you do leave it outside, and give it some winter protection.

The tubers should be planted in a shady situation – at least 10cm (4in) deep in the ground – during autumn.

Separate offsets from mature specimens, and replant during March–April, prior to the growing season.

It is possible, if difficult, to grow from seed but you will need patience, as it takes about five years for the 'flowering' of the spadix and spathe. Sow the freshly collected seeds in pots in the cold frame and think that five years is but a nanosecond when compared to the infinity of extinction.

ARISARUM PROBOSCIDEUM (MOUSE PLANT)

This plant is a native of the southern Mediterranean regions of Spain and Italy. It has a very discreet 6–10cm (2½–4in) spathe with a long tail of dark brown-black hidden beneath the leaves like a timid mouse, hence its common name.

Arisarum proboscideum

However, the Latin name, which is derived from the Greek *proboskis*, relates to the opposite end of the body, referring as it does to a long nose or trunk. The spathe is cowled around a purplish-brown spadix – hence an even smaller, more purple-black-hued relative's common name of 'friar's cowl'.

Best suited to a woodland-style habitat. Propagate in autumn, when the plants are dormant, by carefully dividing the small rhizomes of mature plants.

ARUM

Arum pictum

A Dark Selection

A. dioscoridis Arch 195.157
25cm (10in). A maroon-black spathe with a yellow spadix which appears between May and June. A striking combination. This particular variety is from Turkey.

A. pictum
20cm (8in). The maroon-black flowers appear between September and October. (N.B. Not to be confused with *A. italicum* 'Pictum'.)

Other arums which have dark spotting on lighter-coloured backgrounds include *A. maculatum* 'Pleddel' and *A. dioscoridis* var. *Smithii*. See also *Dracunculus vulgaris* (syn. *A. dracunculus*) on page 35.

GROW HOW

Size: Various.

Season: Various.

Site: Dry, well-drained soil. Partial shade to full sun.

Propagation: Division/Offsets.

This genus of tender perennials is grown for its ornamental leaves and attractive spathes. It is native mainly to the Middle East and eastern Mediterranean.

These are quite tender plants which like dry conditions that mimic their natural habitat. Division of the tuber and separation of offsets should take place when the plants are dormant, i.e. late summer to early autumn.

ASARUM (WILD GINGER)

Like most of the more unusual-looking plants, the asarum originates from the Far East, and new discoveries are still being made. It is a woodland plant which, rather like the mouse plant (see page 28), grows inconspicuously in the undergrowth. Closer examination reveals almost alien-looking lobed flowers with a slightly furry coating hidden under heart-shaped leaves. Asarum provide groundcover, but on a small scale.

Asarum maximum

A Dark Selection

A. maximum
20 x 45cm (8 x 18in). Black flowers with a white heart which are only 6cm (2¼in) diameter.

A. magnificum
Flowers are 4cm (1½in) in diameter and again are black, but this time with a throat of white and pink.

Other dark possibilities include *A. shuttleworthii,* with brown flowers which last longer, from April to July, and *A. splendens* whose colouring is blotchy purple-black and beige.

GROW HOW

Size: Various.

Season: May–June.

Site: Moist, but free-draining, enriched soil. Partial to full shade.

Propagation: Division/Seed/Stolons.

Because of its low height, the asarum is a great temptation to our mollusc friends, so only grow it in a natural habitat if you are prepared for losses. Better instead to keep your specimen plants in pots in a cool conservatory/greenhouse. Whether they are kept outside or indoors, make sure that they are grown in coarse soil with leaf mould to mimic their habitat. Keep the plants fairly dry to prevent root rot, but they will need regular watering to survive. They will also benefit from feeding during the growing season.

Propagation is best from seed, but this really is the domain of the experts. Alternatively, the small rhizomes can be divided in spring. *A. magnificum* can also be propagated by stolons.

BIARUM

This plant is another dark aroid from the Mediterranean, and one which is also malodorous. The dark spathe is not on a stalk, but comes directly out of the ground to be followed later by the leaves. In cooler climes, and also considering its autumnal flowering, it is best suited to a place in the greenhouse and, remembering the smell when it blooms, not the conservatory.

A Dark Selection

B. eximium
This has a purple-black spathe which curves downwards in a backwards arch.

B. tenuifolium
A larger, dark purple spathe and, as the name suggests, narrow leaves.

Biarum tenuifolium

GROW HOW

Size: 10–20cm (4–8in).

Season: Autumn.

Site: Very well-drained to dry, gritty or sandy soil. Full sun.

Propagation: Division/Seed.

Seed can be sown in autumn or spring and will germinate at 13°C (55°F). Division of the tubers, on the other hand, should take place in summer during dormancy, at which time they should be kept dry.

New plants, and newly divided ones, should be planted at least 5cm (2in) deep, and watering should always be on the conservative side.

However, they will need to have regular light waterings when the leaves appear.

B. tenuifolium is the hardier of the two and can therefore be kept outside in a sheltered position which traps the sun, for example at the bottom of a south-facing brick wall.

COSMOS ATROSANGUINEUS (SYN. BIDENS ATROSANGUINEA) (CHOCOLATE COSMOS, BLACK COSMOS)

Originally from Mexico, but no longer found there in the wild, this attractive-looking plant with its distinctive chocolate aroma belongs to the same genus as lettuce.

Cosmos atrosanguineus

GROW HOW

Size: 75cm (29½in).

Season: Late summer.

Site: Well-drained soil. Full sun in a sheltered situation.

Propagation: Cuttings.

Although this perennial is hardy to approximately −5°C (23°F), it is best to treat it as a tender perennial, rather than risking its loss, even if your garden is temperate in winter. If subjected to frequent wet, cold, winters the tuber will just rot away, and a mulch given as winter protection may not be enough.

Although it involves more effort, it is preferable to lift the tuber and store it in dry sand in the warm indoors.

It is also worth taking cuttings just in case, by taking early stem or basal cuttings in late spring to early summer and placing them in a propagator to root.

Protect this plant at all times from slugs and snails, who adore it even more than I do.

DAHLIA

Dahlias were introduced to Europe from central America in the late eighteenth century, by the Swedish botanist Anders Dahl. Such has been the popularity of this vibrant late-flowering plant that there are now over 20,000 known cultivars listed by The Royal Horticultural Society.

A Dark Selection

Border:
D. 'Arabian Night'
120cm (47in). Maroon-black.

D. 'Black Diamond'
100cm (39in). Maroon-black, particularly in the centre of the pom-pom. Almost a blend of burgundy red and black.

Decorative Giant:
D. 'Black Monarch'
120cm (47in). Red-black blooms almost 25cm (10in) in diameter.

There are also several cultivars of dahlia which have almost black leaves; these include 'Bishop of Llandaff' and 'Grenadier' which have red flowers, 'Roxy' with magenta flowers, and 'Tally Ho' with vermillion. A natural hybrid from 'Bishop of Llandaff' has single-flowered chocolate-maroon flowers with yellow stamens, but

Dahlia 'Bishop of Llandaff', a cultivar with black leaves

this one is not commercially available.

Towards the end of May plant out overwintered tubers at least 10cm (4in) deep in rich soil. Dahlias will benefit from a feed, such as bonemeal and phostrogen, to encourage growth. As with the cosmos previously, young shoots are particularly attractive to slugs. They also require staking at the time of planting; this may at first appear unsightly but, whether you use canes, twigs or green plastic-coated staking supports, they should be put in place; this will prevent the development of weak stems and flopping blooms, and the danger of inadvertently piercing and damaging the tubers later on.

Dahlias cannot be propagated from seed as they do not come true. Instead, divide the mature tuber in early spring prior to new growth. You can also take basal cuttings at this time, if not slightly earlier, but remember not to plant the rooted young plants out until all fear of frost has passed, and then make sure to leave enough room for full growth – the planting distance should be as far apart as the final plant is tall. If you want to attain some very large blooms, this will be at the expense of number, as you will need to remove all buds on a stem except the terminal, i.e. the top bud.

It is best to cut back the stems and lift the tubers after flowering, in late autumn. Leave them to dry out, turning them upside down to drain out any water. Overwinter in the warm indoors, placing them in an almost dry sand and peat mixture, with the crowns visible, until it is time to plant them out the following spring.

GROW HOW

Size: Various.

Season: July–October.

Site: Moist, but well-drained, enriched soil. Full sun.

Propagation: Cuttings/Division.

DRACUNCULUS VULGARIS (COMMON DRAGON ARUM)

This is yet another aroid, of the malodorous variety. Of southern Mediterranean origin, including Crete, this is indeed a plant with great presence in terms of its size, smell and appearance.

Fortunately, the carrion-like smell is at its strongest only when the deep burgundy spathe first opens. It surrounds a central narrow spike of a black spadix above a mottled purple-black stem, and palmate leaves grow around and above.

GROW HOW

Size: 90–100x90cm (35–39x35in) spread.
Season: June–July.
Site: Well-drained soil. Full sun to light shade in a sheltered situation.
Propagation: Division/Seed.

A very rare related aroid – *Amorphophallus kiusianus*, a name which leaves nothing to the imagination – has a black spadix surrounded with a brownish-green spathe.

Like most of us, *D. vulgaris* prefers a Mediterranean climate to the cold and wet, and will therefore need winter protection to keep it dry and warm.

The common dragon arum can be propagated by division in late summer, its dormant period, although it can survive division at other times of the year. Gently prise the tubers apart by hand and pot up each one separately. If you place them in a shady site outdoors, they should produce new growth and be ready to plant into the border as early as September or October of the same year. It can also be grown from seed but this is much more difficult, and it will take more than a year to germinate after pre-chilling and sowing in spring.

Dracunculus vulgaris

FRITILLARIA (FRITILLARY)

Fritillary is also the name of a butterfly, which like the most readily recognizable of the fritillaries, *F. meleagris* (snake's-head fritillary) has a chequerboard pattern on its beautiful wings.

A Dark Selection

F. camschatcensis (black sarana, the black lily)
20–40cm (8–16in). Each stem bears clusters of up to eight bell-shaped maroon-black flowers with pale green stamens between May and June.

F. davisii
10–15cm (4–6in). Drooping single purple to brown-black flowers, April to May. Their chequered interior appears to be almost translucent in the spring sunshine.

Fritillaria camschatcensis

F. persica 'Adiyaman'
100cm (39in). As the name implies, this native of the Middle East, has dull maroon-black nodding bell-like flowers on tall stems in late spring.

GROW HOW

Size: Various.

Season: Spring–early summer.

Site: Various.

Propagation: Seed/Offsets.

Some fritillaries, such as *F. camschatcensis*, tolerate or indeed prefer partial to full shade in a moist, rich, acidic, peaty soil. Others like *F. davisii* and *F. persica*, are best suited to full sunshine and well-drained conditions, because of their origins. The small size of *F. davisii* makes it an ideal dry rockery plant, as the habitat will protect it from the damp/wet. Nevertheless you need to make sure that they are all kept well-watered during the flowering period. Cut down the stems after flowering.

Fritillaries can be grown from seed, but they take about five years to reach flowering size and may need cold stratification more than once to kick-start germination. So it is a long-term commitment requiring a degree of expertise but, if you wish to try this, sow the seeds in individual pots containing a sandy mixture, and then cover them lightly with the soil.

From an August sowing with freshly collected seed, it can take up to 18 months before the seedlings can finally be planted out. In any case, don't plant the seedlings out until they are at least a year old, and protect them from direct sunlight during this crucial growing stage. Choose the site of planting out carefully, as they prefer to remain undisturbed for a few years.

Alternatively, you can create more stock by division of the bulbils from the parent bulb after flowering, but don't expect flowers from them in the succeeding season. Scales produced on the bulb can be prised off and planted individually to create new plants; don't remove too many scales or the parent bulb will be depleted, and make sure that the scales so removed are completely intact, as the new bulbs are produced from their bases. They and parent bulbs should be planted on their sides in autumn. Again, like the seed, the scales need a gritty, sandy mixture that provides good drainage. Even propagation with scales requires some

Fritillaria persica 'Adiyaman'

experience to mimic natural conditions and induce germination, which can take up to six months.

GLADIOLUS

So named after its sword-shaped leaves (Latin – *gladius)*, this plant originates from the continent of Africa. As well as being a border plant, it can be grown as a pot plant indoors, for brightening up the winter gloom.

A Dark Selection

G. *atroviolaceus* 'Ebony Beauty'
Almost black – violet-black.

G. *splendens* 'Sweet Shadow'
Burgundy-black flowers combined with dark leaves, from August to September.

G. *atrioviolaceus* (from the Middle East) is a good plant for the British climate as – provided it is situated in a sheltered site – it is hardier than most other gladioli. But, as with many bulbous plants which are native to warmer climes, the corms should be dug up and overwintered indoors in dry conditions. Plant them out again in spring – in soil enriched with some manure and/or bonemeal, if yours is poor – when the earth has started to warm. Plant corms to a depth of 10cm (4in), on top of sand to improve

GROW HOW
Size: 60–70cm ($23\frac{1}{2}$–$27\frac{1}{2}$in).
Season: Summer to autumn.
Site: Free-draining soil with plenty of sand or grit. Full sun..
Propagation: Offcuts.

drainage, and space them about 25cm (10in) apart to allow plenty of room for growth. If planting in an open site it is a wise precaution to put in stakes at the same time, as the stems may not be strong enough to take the weight of the flowers.

Gladioli corms produce a lot of 'offspring' which can be easily removed from the parent and planted in March to produce more stock; these will reach flowering size in one to three years.

At the same time of year, it is possible to grow gladioli from seed, sown shallowly; the seeds should germinate in about a month and will then take the same amount of time to reach maturity.

HEMEROCALLIS (DAYLILY)

Each flower of the daylily only lasts a day, so it is aptly named from the Greek: *hemere* (day) *kallos* (beauty). It originated in Asia, where it was especially popular in China for its culinary and medicinal uses, reaching Europe in the sixteenth century.

Daylilies are categorized by flower size, flowering period and height. A complex language has also developed to describe their wide range of hues and patterning.

Modern American breeders in particular have improved the range and quality of cultivars, but many of these are neither suitable nor available for the UK climate. Those listed, however, can survive in sheltered sites, or harsher situations if treated as half-hardy.

A Dark Selection

H. 'American Revolution'
Maroon-black.

H. 'Black Magic'
Red-black.

H. 'Brunette'
Small mahogany flowers.

H. 'Night Beacon'
Red-black.

H. 'Root Beer'
Flushed maroon.

H. 'Siloam Sambo'
Small red-black flowers.

Daylilies can suffer in wet, cold winters, but cannot be overwintered indoors – unless they are planted in containers – as their roots should not be disturbed. Instead, give them a thick dry mulch to protect them from crown rot.

In spring, dig in manure, avoiding crowns, to enrich the soil and improve flowering. Deadhead regularly and, after flowering is over, cut back the stems to just above ground level.

GROW HOW

Size: 75–100cm (29½–39½in)

Season: July–September (except 'Brunette' which flowers from May).

Site: Fertile soil which must not be alkaline. Full sun to partial shade.

Propagation: Division/Offsets/Seed.

Hemerocallis 'Black Magic'

Daylilies can be propagated by division every three years or so in spring or late summer, but only by two or three, as more will reduce the plants' chances of survival.

Although they can be grown from seed, it is a process for the experienced and equipped gardener, and those not grown under clinical conditions are not always true to the parent plant; this would be a major disappointment, as the germination period alone can be anything up to a year and should be preceded by a cold stratification period of at least six weeks. It can then be up to four years until that beautiful day when a plant produces its first flowers.

It is easier, though just as long-term an endeavour, to produce more plants from bulb scales after flowering. Don't remove too many scales, or you will deplete the vigour of the parent rhizome. Plant the scales in a gritty, light mixture.

New growth is attractive to pests such as slugs and greenfly, so keep a watchful eye.

HERMODACTYLUS TUBEROSUS (SYN. IRIS TUBEROSA) (WIDOW IRIS)

This plant has a separate entry because, although it looks like a beardless iris (see picture), it does in fact belong, like hemerocallis, to the lily family.

This iris has black velvety falls and partially striped green standards during spring. Because it likes a dry, limey situation in sun, it would be a worthwhile addition to a rockery or alpine garden. Keep it away from wet, damp conditions.

Divide mature plants in late summer, during the dormant period.

Hermodactylus tuberosus

GROW HOW

Size: 25–30cm (10–12in).

Season: February–May.

Site: Very well-drained, sandy, alkaline soil. Full sun to partial shade.

Propagation: Division.

IRIS CHRYSOGRAPHES (BEARDLESS IRIS)

Iris chrysographes 'Black Night'

A Dark Selection

I. chrysographes 'Black Night'
45–60cm (17½–24in). Deep purple, almost black.

I. chrysographes 'Black Forms'
45cm (17½in). Deep maroon to almost black.

I. chrysographes 'Inshriach'
45cm (17½in). Almost black.

I. chrysographes prefers a shady, moist habitat especially when germinating, and can even be used as a marginal plant near a pond. Seeds need pre-soaking and pre-chilling to coax them to germinate, which can take from a month to as long as a year and a half. Preferably divide when dormant to propagate.

The beardless iris originated in China and, with its lovely delicate flowers which feature wispily drooping narrow falls, it is perhaps rather less familiar than the wonderfully billowy and ruffled appearance displayed by the bearded iris (see page 42).

GROW HOW

Size: 45–60cm (17½–24in).

Season: May–June.

Site: Moist soil. Full sun to full shade.

Propagation: Division/Seed.

IRIS (BEARDED OR FLAG IRIS)

The bearded iris or flag iris is probably the most familiar floral image after that of the sunflower, both finding fame through the paintings of Van Gogh, and to a lesser extent Claude Monet. Pliny the Elder, the Roman naturalist historian, claimed that one of the beneficial uses of the iris (although he doesn't specify the part) was that when it was chewed it sweetened 'foul breath and offensive armpits' as well as aiding against more unpleasant ailments.

Named after the ancient Greek goddess of the rainbow, the varieties of iris from which our modern bearded varieties were originally cultivated came from Greece, Persia and Eastern Europe; today it is principally the American growers who are most renowned for producing fantastically beautiful new cultivars and hybrids.

However, they still struggle to produce a true red iris, though *I. caerulea* 'Caliente' with its red-maroon colouring, is perhaps one of the most striking near-misses. However, in contrast to breeders of the tulip, they have produced many black and almost black cultivars, of which those listed below are but a selection.

The bearded iris can be generally classified into three sizes and flowering seasons (although the British Iris Society actually uses six): Dwarf (D), 25–40cm (10–16in), flowering from mid- to late May for up to a month; Tall (T), 100–120cm (39–47in), flowering during either the first or second half of June; and Intermediate (I), 60–90cm (23½–35½in) which, as a hybrid of the Tall and Dwarf, has an overlapping season from late May to late June.

It is difficult to categorize some of the examples as either black or purple-black, as the latter often have an efflorescent quality which, at a certain distance and in certain light conditions, makes them appear much blacker than they really are; *I. ruthenica* 'Sable' is an example of this but, for a selective list, see the facing page.

Iris 'Black Swan'

Iris pumila 'Dark Vader'

A Dark Selection

True Black:
I. 'Deep Black' (I)
I. 'Helen Proctor' (I)
I. 'Superstition' (I)
I. 'Swazi Princess' (I)

Blue-Black:
I. 'Black Hills' (T)
I. 'Black Knight' (T)

Purple-Black:
I. 'Black Swan' (I)
I. 'Black Watch' (I)
I. 'Dark Vader' (D)
I. 'Dusky Dancer' (I)
I. 'Interpol' (I)
I. 'Jewel Baby' (D)
I. 'Little Black Belt' (D)
I. 'Midnight Madness' (D)
I. 'Raven Hill' (I)
I. 'Sable' (I)
I. 'Sweet Treat' (D)

Red-Black:
I. 'Langport Wren' (I)
I. 'Ruby Mine' (I)
I. 'Solid Mahogany' (I)

Bicolour:
I. Brown-Black/Red
I. 'Louvois' (I)

Brown-Black yellow:
I. 'Staten Island' (I)

Other dark varieties of the iris for the enthusiastic gardener include the aril iris (Regeliocyclus hybrid) 'Clotho', which suits alpine conditions, and the marginal *Iris ensata* (Japanese water iris) 'The Great Moghul', and the Lousiana hybrid 'Black Gamecock'.

GROW HOW

Size: Various.

Season: May and/or June.

Site: Well-drained neutral to alkaline, even chalky soil. Full sun to partial shade.

Propagation: Division/Seed (the latter for species only).

Irises do not like to be disturbed, so take care in selecting the right site from the start and, if you have acidic soil, add an alkaline agent such as lime. Tall varieties need a warm, sunny site, but Intermediate and Dwarf sizes will do as well in partial shade and cooler climes. Leave enough room for growth, which for the Tall means a 60cm (24in) circumference.

Iris ensata

If your garden is subject to regular aphid and rust attacks, it is advisable to choose either a Dwarf or Intermediate iris which has more resistance to disease.

The rhizomes should be lightly covered and, if planted in heavy soil, also set above ground level, slightly showing their crowns. If set too deep, rot can set in, too high and they can wither and dry out. They do best in a well-drained, but not dry, neutral to slightly alkaline soil. If your garden soil is particularly heavy, dig in some gritty sand and, if desired, some leaf mould.

As it is with most flowers, deadheading prolongs the flowering season, but don't do it if you want to collect the seed! Irises can be grown from seed sown in the autumn but both germination and growth are very slow. When flowering is over, cut the stems down to the base. This is also the time to use a low-nitrogen/high-potash fertilizer if you need to. Avoid using manure, unless it is well rotted and, if used, make sure it doesn't come into contact with the rhizome.

Propagation is best undertaken by division, soon after flowering, and no later than the end of September. To maintain the quality of flowering and plant shape you should anyway divide the plant into two or three healthy sections with roots and shoot every three years.

You may find that new rhizomes have grown and taken over from a less healthy parent, which should be discarded. To help the new plants re-establish themselves, cut down the leaves to a third of their height.

LEPTINELLA ATRATA (SYN. *COTULA ATRATA*)

This member of the aster family is easy to grow as a rockery or groundcover plant. It has evergreen fern-like foliage, and tiny 1cm (½in) diameter daisy-like black-red flowers which appear totally black in the centre until all the sepals open to reveal yellow stamens that take over as the flowers age. Sow ripe seed in the flowering position, divide established clumps and replant after flowering is over.

GROW HOW

Size: 15 x 20cm (6 x 8in) spread.

Season: May–July.

Site: Well-drained, gritty yet fertile soil. Full sun.

Propagation: Division/Seed.

OPHRYS FUSCA (BEE ORCHID)

This is a deciduous, frost-hardy, terrestial orchid, of European origin. In spring it produces spikes of greenish, yellow or brown flowers, each with a yellow-edged, bluish, brown-black or purple lip.

Another darkish variety is *O. insectifera* (fly orchid). With their hairy lips/beards both of these have some resemblance to the insect world, as their common names imply.

No orchid likes wet, cold conditions, as this causes the tubers to rot. But, equally, it is important to make sure that they don't dry out completely in the summer months.

GROW HOW

Size: 100cm (39in).

Season: May–August.

Site: Moist, fertile soil. Full sun to partial shade.

Propagation: Division/Seed.

Ophrys fusca

SANGUISORBA OFFICINALIS (GREATER BURNET)

This clump-forming, perennial plant is fully hardy. It is native to the damp meadows of Europe and North America and is ideally suited to the wildflower garden/meadow. Its maroon-black flowers are in densely packed spikes which resemble small bottlebrushes.

Seed from *S. officinalis* can be sown in autumn under glass for planting out in spring, or sown in position in spring. It is also possible to propagate by division of the rhizome at this time. It reaches 1.2m (4ft) high so – unless you are aiming for a naturally wild effect – it's advisable to stake the plants to ensure a tidy border .

Another characteristic of this plant is that it can be invasive. This means that you could be faced with the prospect of obliterating plants rather than propagating them!

GROW HOW

Size: 120cm (4ft).

Season: May–August.

Site: Moist, fertile soil. Full sun to partial shade.

Propagation: Division/Seed.

TRILLIUM (TRINITY FLOWER, WOOD LILY)

Trillium chloropetalum

This delicately-flowered perennial, found in the woodlands of North America, has several dark varieties but remember that, if the petals become blacker, it is a warning sign for disease.

However desirable these trilliums may be to you, do some digging around at nurseries, as they are of course not to be dug up from the wild.

A Dark Selection

T. *chloropetalum*
30–45cm(12–18in). Red-black flowers appear later than most (March–May).

T. *reliquum*
18cm(7in). Brown-purple malodorous and rare blooms above slightly mottled leaves (March–April).

T. *stamineum* 'Harbison'
20cm (8in). Twisted dark purple petals smelling of carrion (March–April).

T. *underwoodii*
8–20cm (3–8in). Maroon-black above marbled leaves (February – March).

Propagation from seed sown in autumn is possible, but difficult. Sow seed as soon as it is ripe, because if it's stored it is unlikely to germinate ever. Even then, seedlings can take two years to appear, and then between four to seven years to reach maturity. Instead, divide the rhizomes of established plants in summer, after the foliage has died down, or let them slowly spread naturally. All will grow well in woodland conditions in moist soil, except T. *stamineum* 'Harbison', which prefers its woods to be dry.

GROW HOW

Size: Various.

Season: Spring.

Site: Well-drained, yet leaf mould enriched, neutral soil. Partial to full shade.

Propagation: Division/Seed.

Trillium chloropetalum (close up)

TULIPA (TULIP)

The tulip was introduced to Europe in the sixteenth century from Turkey, where spring festivals are still held in its honour. This vibrant, mainly spring-flowering bulb, comes in many varieties and colours, except for blue – unlike the iris. The black tulip, 'widow-like beneath a sable veil' has special significance (see Introduction, page 4).

Tulipa 'Queen of Night'

The tulip is also linked with the fairies by both the Persians and Hans Christian Andersen, who has his Thumbelina floating down a stream in a tulip petal.

There are 15 official classifications of tulip. These are based on its size, the shape of the flower and the flowering season.

A Dark Selection

T. 'Black Parrot'
50cm (20in) Maroon-ish tinge to purple-black flowers in May. The 'Parrot' refers to the feathered, jagged appearance of the petals. (See picture on facing page.)

T. 'Black Swan'
60–70cm (23–28in). Purple-black flowers from early to mid-May. The petal colours become more distinct with age. (See p. 49.)

T. 'Queen of Night'
60–70cm (23–28). Velvety purplish tinge to black 'traditional' shaped blooms which appear in May. (See picture on left.)

Another cultivar, which is a bicolour, is 'Gavota', which is smaller at 45cm (18in) and has maroon-black flowers edged with hues of creamy yellow in April to May, i.e. mid-season.

These mid-season and late tulips are more tolerant of exposed positions and poor weather conditions.

GROW HOW

Size: Various.

Season: Various.

Site: Almost any as long as there is good drainage, but best in slightly alkaline soil. Sheltered situation. Full sun.

Propagation: Division/Seed.

Tulipa 'Black Swan'

Whether tulips should be treated in the same way as daffodils, and the foliage be allowed to die back to replenish the bulb, is debatable: most gardeners believe that doing this increases the risk of disease to the plant itself and the surrounding soil. Instead, remove the seed pods to stop all the strength of the plant being used up in reproduction. Once the leaves have yellowed, they and the stems should be cut right back and burnt or discarded, and the dropped petals cleared from the ground. Do not compost the remains.

Ideally, bulbs should be lifted every year after flowering – particularly if drainage is not very good – and stored in a cool place in net bags to allow air to circulate. Realistically, most of us have neither the time nor the inclination to do this so, if you plan to leave them in the ground, plant them approximately half as deep again as recommended, i.e. 10cm (4in) deep and 12–15cm (4¾–6in) apart. To achieve the best effect, plant them in groups.

The most important consideration when planting tulips is to find a good site which will reduce the risk of disease. You should avoid waterlogged sites. New bulbs, or old bulbs in new locations (they should be moved every few years) can be planted as late as November; indeed the later they are planted the better.

It is possible to grow tulips from seed, if you like a challenge. But bear in mind they can take up to a year to germinate after being sown in the cold frame in autumn.

Tulipa 'Black Parrot'

VERATRUM NIGRUM (BLACK FALSE HELLEBORE)

Veratrum nigrum

The name of this perennial (like that of the black hellebore proper) actually refers to the colour of the root. This plant also has purple-black flowers on fork-like spikes and large and waxy ribbed leaves, resembling those of the hosta. They are best planted away from the house or patio, as they have a rather pungent smell that is only attractive to insects.

GROW HOW

Size: 1.5m x 60cm (59 x 24in) spread.

Season: August–September.

Site: Peaty, moist soil. Sheltered site. Semi-to full shade.

Propagation: Cuttings/Division/Seed.

To propagate, divide the rhizomes in autumn or spring. Alternatively, take root cuttings with a bud above, and then root in a well-drained, sandy mixture in a cold frame. Seeds can be sown in autumn or spring also, but can you really bear to wait 10 years for a full-sized plant?

To encourage these plants to thrive, it's a good idea to cut them back in autumn.

ZANTEDESCHIA (CALLA OR ARUM LILY)

Named after the nineteenth-century Italian botanist Giovanni Zantedeschi, this usually evergreen perennial lily has its origins in South Africa, but it is also naturalized elsewhere. The cultivar 'Schwarzwalder' has a dramatic glossy black spathe edged in red, surrounded by wavy, waxy leaves speckled with white.

Zantedeschia is a versatile and long-flowering plant that will cope with both shade and sun. It needs protection and warmth to do well so, in many climes, a cool greenhouse or conservatory rather than an outdoor site is best, although it could cope in a sheltered part of the garden. If it is planted outside, it will need covering over with a dry mulch during the cold months, as it is not frost hardy.

GROW HOW

Size: 50cm (20in).

Season: June–September.

Site: Loam-based, sandy soil. Sheltered site. Full sun to full shade.

Propagation: Division.

Zantedeschia 'Schwarzwalder'

FLOWERS

HARDY PERENNIALS

AQUILEGIA (COLUMBINE)

Both the Latin and common name are bird related: to the diametrically opposed eagle and the dove (the latter from *columba*). The columbine often features as a symbolic reference to God in Renaissance paintings.

A Dark Selection

A. *atrata*
30–60cm (12–24in). A quite rare variety from the Alps; almost black with yellow stamens.

A. *viridiflora*
30cm (12in). A fragrant alpine variety with a purple-black centre and outer petals of an unusual grey-brown, with large spurs and contrasting yellow-green anthers.

A. *vulgaris* 'William Guiness' aka 'Magpie'
60–80cm (24–32in). Black and white, like the drink, but apparently not named after the brewers.

A. *vulgaris* 'Black Barlow'
60–90cm (24–35½in). The frilly 'Granny Bonnet' type with purple-black petals and yellow centre.

A. *vulgaris* 'Double Black Maroon'
85cm (33in) The description says it all.

Aquilegia atrata

GROW HOW

Size: Various.

Season: May–June.

Site: Any soil, preferably moist but well-drained (except *A. viridiflora* which requires a free-draining, gritty site). Full sun to partial shade.

Propagation: Division/Seed.

Once planted, try not to disturb the plants but if you must – e.g. to divide the rhizomes of any older, established plants which have become less floriferous – do so in spring.

Sowing and self-seeding is a less disruptive method to replace tired plants; however, as aquilegia hybridize easily, you will need to remove and discard seedheads of the more dominant *A. vulgaris* if planted near other varieties, in order to keep your stock pure.

Sow the collected seed in autumn or spring (if the latter, pre-chill the seed), in pots for planting out when the weather warms. The seeds are extremely fine, so leave them uncovered. They take quite a long time to germinate – even occasionally more than three months – and the temperature needs to be least 18°C (64°F); if nothing has appeared after three months, you may need to chill the seeds again, to fool the biological clock. Once they start, however, they will go from strength to strength.

Aquilegia vulgaris 'William Guiness'

When ready, plant out at intervals of 30cm (12in), thus allowing for final growth.

ERIGERON SPECIOSUS (FLEABANE)

Erigeron 'Schwarzes Meer'

Daisy-like flowers from North America. A fully hardy, clump-forming perennial. They are good for rock gardens or will look handsome in herbaceous borders.

A Dark Selection

'*E. Darkest of All*'
Blue-black flowers.

E. 'Schwarzes Meer'
Violet-black semi-double flowers.

Erigeron starts flowering in early summer and, if you deadhead the plant, you will be rewarded with a second flush of flowers.

Cut right back in autumn, unless you want it to self-seed. Otherwise, collect seeds and sow them in the cold frame the following April–May and plant them out in autumn in anticipation of flowers the following summer. Alternatively, divide established clumps in spring or early autumn.

GROW HOW

Size: 40cm (16in).

Season: June–August.

Site: Moist, fertile soil. Full sun.

Propagation: Division/Seed.

GERANIUM (CRANESBILL)

Of European origin. The common name 'cranesbill' is a direct translation of the Ancient Greek, and refers to the central protuberance in the small flowers, which is particularly noticeable in the *G. phaeum* variety. This clump-forming perennial, whose flowers rise above the leaves in termainal clusters, is a pretty tough plant that slugs won't touch, and it is easy to propagate successfully.

A Dark Selection

G. *phaeum* 'Mourning Widow'
60cm (24in). Dusky, purple-black flowers in May–June. Some plants have purple marking on the leaves as well.

G. *phaeum* 'Samobor'
35cm (14in). Brown-purple leaves and flowers April–June.

G. *phaeum* 'Variegatum'
45cm (18in). Similar flowers to above, but the leaves are a combination of green, cream and red.

G. *pyrenaicum* 'Bill Wallis'
40cm (16in). Very dark violet-black flowers April–October.

G. *sinensis* 'Halloween'
40cm (16in). Similar to *G. phaeum* 'Mourning Widow' in general appearance, but this is rarer, because of the more vibrant contrast of maroon-black petals, and a central scarlet 'bill' which has hints of pinky white at the base.

Geranium phaeum

There are also geraniums with dark foliage, for example the low-growing 10cm (4in) *Geranium* x *sessiliflorum* 'Nigricans'; this has brown-black leaves, which fade to pale orange when dying, and white flowers. Also *Geranium* Crûg Strain (20cm/8in) whose leaves are browner in colour and which has pale pink flowers. These prefer sunshine to shade, flower from June to November, and are not as hardy.

GROW HOW

Size: Various.

Season: Various.

Site: Any soil. Sun to full shade.

Propagation: Cuttings/Division/Seed.

Seed collected from *G. phaeum* can be sown in pots, or stored for 3–4 weeks in a refrigerator; germination usually occurs in approximately two weeks and seedlings should be planted out between September and March.

Geranium phaeum 'Samobor' (leaves only)

Some species are more difficult than others, and may not produce flowers in the first year. To increase the chance of flowers in the following year, take root cuttings at or just below ground level in spring. The potted root cuttings should initially be kept in the shade. For more flowers in the same year, divide established plants in early spring before they break dormancy. You can divide them also after flowering, in late summer. Division is anyway advisable every few years, to ensure that the quality of the plant is maintained.

Cut back the leaf growth in late summer, leaving enough to protect the crown of the plant over winter. Remove excess leaves to reduce the risk of mildew/rust developing. Alternatively cut back in early spring, just before new growth starts to appear.

HELLEBORUS ORIENTALIS (HELLEBORE)

As mentioned earlier (see pages 4–5), the hellebore certainly has dark connections as well as dark varieties. The plant has been extensively hybridized to produce many subtle variations in petal shape, shading and spotting, and nectaries. All the subtleties of the flowers can be seen by peering up into their drooping heads, and some growers remove the large trifoliate leaves to make them more visible. The hellebore is an attractive clump-forming perennial, which looks even better when light and dark hybrids are planted near to one another.

Dark Varieties & Cultivars

Most of the cultivars belong to specific groups of hybrids or strains, and many are only given a number that signifies the parentage of the plant, an example being the Ashwood Hybrids which include the elusive doubles, as well as purple-blacks, blue-backs and greys, some of which have striking nectaries of yellow, green or red.

By contrast, most of the Eric Smith Strains have been named, some after planets: 'Pluto', 'Saturn' and 'Neptune'. Other dark maroon to purple-blacks include 'Blue Spray', 'Tom Wilson', 'Dusk' and 'Nocturne'.

Then there are the Ballard Hybrids 'Black Knight' and 'Ballard's Black' both of which are very rare. The black-purple 'Sorcerer' is bred in the USA, and there are some more dark hybrids that are only available in mainland Europe, namely the blue-black 'Mitternachts-blues' and also the red-black 'Gewitternacht' and 'Schwarzes Gold'.

Helleborus orientalis Ballard's Group

GROW HOW

Size: 45cm (18in).

Season: February–March.

Site: Rich, moist yet free-draining soil which is not peat-based. Full sun or full shade.

Propagation: Division/Seed.

As the hellebore cross-pollinates and self-seeds easily, cut off the flower stems before the seedheads have formed to retain your original stock. Unless you want to go to the trouble of protecting the flowers and hand pollinating them yourself, you can retain the variety, and multiply those that you want to retain in your garden, by dividing the rhizomes in early autumn.

If you are growing new plants from seed, it must be collected and sown straight away under cover for best results. You need to mimic outdoor conditions, i.e. the cold winter months, to encourage germination. Seeds are slow to germinate and need at least a month or two of cold stratification to start the process, and even a second session, after which they will take two to three years to reach flowering size. The relatively new double cultivars can still produce single flowers, and all can produce flowers of different shades; it takes the patience of the expert breeder to attain a constant and non-reverting strain.

If you are not so fussy, look out for self-seeded seedlings; when these are of a transplantable size, they can be moved to the desired position, after which they should not be disturbed.

Helleborus orientalis Ashwood Garden hybrids

LYSIMACHIA ATROPURPUREA (LOOSESTRIFE)

Originating in the Balkans, this variety of lysimachia has spikes of dark purple-black flowers which are particularly dark in bud. As it is a short-lived perennial (a maximum of two to three years), you will need to propagate new plants from seed regularly. See also *L. ciliata* (page 88) for a dark-leaved example of lysimachia .

Sow the seed in the autumn in a heated propagator, but make sure the maximum temperature does not exceed 18°C (64°F). You can expect your new seedlings to emerge before Christmas, but you should also be prepared to wait until late winter/early spring.

Plant out young plants from October through to April.

Cut back the growth of established plants before winter sets in.

GROW HOW

Size: 80cm (32in).

Season: Early summer.

Site: Moist soil, including marginal situation. Full sun to partial shade.

Propagation: Seed.

Lysimachia atropurpurea

MELIANTHUS MAJOR (HONEYBUSH)

The honeybush, from South Africa, reaches full size in one year and has attractive grey-green foliage and spikes of dark chocolate flowers. This plant is aromatic and attractive to insects. It is evergreen only in the most sheltered sites.

To propagate, you can sow seed, remove suckers and pot them in spring, or take stem-tip cuttings in summer. To protect *M. major* from diseases and pests during the early stages of growth, ensure the stem is covered by several centimetres of soil.

Melianthus major

GROW HOW

Size: 120cm (47in).

Season: May–July.

Site: Moist, well-drained soil – poor soil for the best flowers. Full sun to partial shade.

Propagation: Cuttings/Seed/Suckers.

It will need full frost protection to survive the winter, but if the leaves do get frost damaged despite protection, cut it back and new growth will shoot up in spring.

PENSTEMON

This good-value plant, with long-flowering spires, has dark cultivars that can fill a sizeable gap in any border.

A Dark Selection

P. 'Midnight'
Purple-black.

P. 'Raven'
Purple-black with a hint of maroon and a delicate white throat.

In a sheltered area, the penstemon can survive a few winters, but the flowering capacity does diminish quite obviously as the plant ages. Propagate regularly to replace older or frost-damaged plants, either by taking cuttings in autumn or dividing established clumps in spring.

Cut the plant back in spring to encourage fresh new growth. Cutting back at this time also means that last year's growth, together with a mulch, can help protect the plant from frosts. Even if affected, frost-damaged stems can be removed without ruining the plant.

GROW HOW

Size: 100cm (39in).

Season: June–October.

Site: Well-drained, fertile, moist soil. Full sun.

Propagation: Cuttings/Division.

Although the penstemon is quite hardy, it will need regular watering during the summer months to ensure that it thrives.

Penstemon 'Raven'

PHYTEUMA NIGRA (HORNED RAMPION)

This fully hardy perennial has slightly raggedy spiky balls of purple-black flowers. The Ancient Greek medics claimed it had aphrodisiac qualities.

Because of its preference for dry and sunny conditions, it makes a good rockery plant.

Sow seed in autumn, and protect young plants from slugs and snails. The most effective eco-friendly method is to sink jars of beer up to their necks in the ground, close to the relevant plants. Surrounding the base of the plant with broken eggshells (or soot) can also work, or pellets can be bought which are not harmful to animals.

GROW HOW

Size: 25cm (10in).

Season: Summer.

Site: Very well-drained, neutral to alkaline soil. Full sun.

Propagation: Seed.

Phyteuma nigra

PRIMULA AURICULA (BEAR'S EAR)

The auricula is an alpine species from the large genus of primula. It's been known and loved – and even been an object of obsession – since Huguenot immigrants introduced it into Britain in the sixteenth century. Like so many plants at that time, it had its medicinal uses, but found its greatest popularity in the late eigtheenth century and the Victorian era, which saw a proliferation of shows, societies and strictly judged competitions devoted to this early spring-flowering plant.

Primula auricula 'Haffner'

The auricula is split into categories: Alpine, Border, Double and Show, the last of which is further subdivided into Selfs (one even colour), Edged and Fancy (which includes Borders and Stripes). The Selfs produce most of the dark-coloured cultivars, very popular in the late nineteenth century.

A Dark Selection

Double:
P. a. 'Matthew Yates'
Black-purple with a slightly farinaceous quality.

Edged:
P. a. 'Lee's Colonel Taylor'
Black with green edging (no longer available).

P. a. 'Lee Paul'
Mahogany with gold edging.

Many Edged cultivars have a black outer margin of varying depths to the central

white paste; these include 'Green Jacket', 'Haffner' and 'True Briton', the latter of which has been in existence since 1895.

Selfs:
P. a. 'Hardy Amies'
P .a. 'Nocturne'
P. a. 'Rosalind'
P. a. 'The Mikado'
P. a. 'The Snods'

GROW HOW

Size: 15cm.(6in).

Season: March–May.

Site: Well-drained, gritty but rich soil. Partial shade, avoiding full sun.

Propagation: Cuttings/Division/Offsets.

Because the auricula is of alpine origin, it is hardy to –14 °C (5°F), so it is not a plant for the warm conservatory or the greenhouse. It likes well-drained conditions, especially during the winter, but don't allow it to dry out in the summer, or even when flowering is completely over.

It is prone to pests and diseases, but you can reduce the risk of these by removing dead flowers and leaves, and dividing every two or three years when dormant. The leaves are evergreen and require a cool and shady spot, as do the flowers if you wish to prolong them. Avoid planting in permanently damp areas, to avoid root rot.

Seed-grown plants will not be true to the parent, but you may still enjoy propagating them in this way. If you wish to try, collect the seeds in July and store them in cool conditions; the following February, sow the seeds in pots in a mixture which initially includes at least a quarter of sand or grit for drainage. Place under glass. These seed-grown plants will not flower in their first year, and it is important to keep the young plants shaded at all times until they are established. They will benefit from a yearly application of bonemeal, particularly if they are grown outdoors.

RUDBECKIA (CONEFLOWER)

Named after the Swedish botanists, the Olaf Rudbecks, the rudbeckia is most often identified with the hot-coloured late summer border, as most cultivars are in golden-yellow to orange hues. The cultivar 'Green Wizard' is an exception. Though its name places the emphasis on the green sepals (not petals) which surround the central cone, it is this cone of black florets that merits inclusion in this selection.

GROW HOW

Size: 120–150cm (47–59in).

Season: July–October.

Site: Moist, but not waterlogged, rich soil. Full sun.

Propagation: Cuttings/Division/Seed.

Rudbeckia 'Green Wizard'

If growing from seed, don't expect all seedlings to come true. Sow the seed in early spring and grow on for planting out in October. Seed can, however, take up to three months to germinate, so don't expect flowers in the first year. Once established, propagation is then easier by division under-taken approximately every two years in spring. It is also possible to take basal stem cuttings. Watch out for slugs and snails.

SALVIA (SAGE)

There are over 900 species of salvia, and the dark examples given below span three continents. The sage has been prized for its healing qualities since Roman times, if not before, hence the Latin name from *salvare* – to save. Leaves of some species are used for flavouring food.

Salvia x *sylvestris* 'Mainacht'

A Dark Selection

S. castanea
Brown-black flowers. From China.

S. discolor
Blue-black flowers emerging from silver-green calyxes above aromatic foliage. This plant, from Peru, has tendrils and needs staking support.

S. x sylvestris '**Mainacht**'
This has violet-black flowers on nearly black calyxes and stems. From Germany.

For dark foliage, try *S. spathacea* from California. This species provides dark purple to maroon, artichoke-shaped leaves, which are spaced up the stems, and from which deep pink flowers protrude.

Most salvias need a good mulch to help them survive the harsher winters, but *S. sylvestris*, because of its European woodland origin, is hardier than most and can even cope with a little shade. Nevertheless, it's a good idea to take a few softwood cuttings during the growing period and to root them in fairly dry conditions in the greenhouse, so that they will be ready for planting out the following year. Seed can be sown *in situ* in spring.

Like the mint to which it is related, sage can be quite invasive, so it's a good idea to grow this plant in pots for placing on the patio, or sinking into the border where the confines of the pot will prevent spreading. Also, remember to remove the flowerheads before they have a chance to disperse their seed. Make sure the plants are all kept well watered during hot spells.

GROW HOW

Size: 90–120cm (3–4ft).

Season: May–August.

Site: Well-drained, humus enriched soil. Full sun.

Propagation: Cuttings/Seed.

VIOLA CORNUTA (VIOLET)

The violet was popular as a motif of love from Elizabethan to Victorian times. As the species is naturally purple, it has been relatively easy to produce darker hues that eventually reached the colour black itself. However, it is possible that black strains revert, especially as they cross-pollinate very easily.

Viola cornuta 'Rocastle Black'

A Dark Selection

V. c. 'Black from Black'
V. c. 'Black Jack'
V. c. Midnight Runner'
V. c. 'Molly Sanderson'
V. c. 'Painted Black'
V. c. 'Penny Black'
V. c. 'Rocastle Black'
V. c. 'Sawyer's Black'

For dark foliage try *V. riviniana* Purpurea Group, which has dark purplish-black leaves and violet-blue flowers. See also under *V.* x *wittrokiana* (pansy) in the Annuals section (page 26).

If you're sowing seed, rather than dividing established clumps, it can aid germination to place the seed in the refrigerator for a couple of weeks; then sow in trays and place these in a humid dark place to await the appearance of seedlings. If you make repeat sowings, each a couple of weeks apart, you will have long-lasting flowers for planting in window boxes, containers, and mixing in the front of the border. Sow seed indoors from February, and plant out between April and late June, or sow outdoors in June.

It is possible to prolong the flowering of your violets to six months of the year, if you remember to deadhead the plants regularly.

GROW HOW

Size: 10–15cm (4–6in).
Season: April–September.
Site: Almost any.
Propagation: Division/Seed.

FOLIAGE

ANNUALS, BIENNIALS AND TENDER PERENNIALS

ACALYPHA WILKESIANA (COPPERLEAF, JACOB'S COAT)

Acalypha wilkesiana 'Can Can'

This tender evergreen perennial, found in the South Pacific Islands as well as in Indonesia and Malaysia, can grow to be a monster of a plant 3m (9ft) tall. It makes an unusual addition to the conservatory, as it is covered from top to bottom in almost black leaves, edged with cerise, which eclipse the small racemes of flowers. The oil from the seed is a very strong emetic.

Water this plant well during the summer, and pinch out the tips of growing stems to promote bushier growth. Copperleaf can be propagated by taking softwood or semi-ripe cuttings in the summer.

GROW HOW

Size: Up to 3m (9ft 10in).

Season: Evergreen.

Site: Well-drained, humus rich soil. Likes partial shade.

Propagation: Cuttings.

Codiaeum variegatum belongs to the same family of Euphorbiaceae; it is more multi-coloured in appearance but likes similar conditions. Unnamed cultivars of this can be found which have very dark leaves, often combining black with shades of pink.

AEONIUM ARBOREUM 'SCHWARZKOPF'

Sometimes translated from the German as 'Black Cap' (though strictly speaking it should be 'Head'), this succulent from the Canary Islands, with its distinctive and striking rosettes of burnt black foliage, is very easy to grow, and can reach its maximum size in as little as five years.

GROW HOW

Size: Up to 90cm (3ft).

Season: Evergreen.

Site: Well-drained, gritty, loam-based soil. Full but not harsh sun.

Propagation: Cuttings.

Even though it is a succulent, the aeonium will tolerate English summers outdoors, and a temperature of 10°C (50°F) indoors during the colder months. You will need to bring it indoors during the winter, unless you can be sure that your garden's climate will neither drop below about 13°C (55°F), nor suffer frosts. For this reason, it is best to keep it as a container plant.

It is easy to propagate by taking stem-tip or leaf cuttings and pushing them a couple of centimetres down into dry soil in small pots; rooting will then occur in a few weeks. New growth is sometimes greener than that on the established plant. A greener leaf colour is also an indication that the plant is being overwatered and, as with all succulents and many other indoor plants, watering should always be reduced during dormant or colder periods.

Stems can become quite tall, but a fuller shape, with more rosettes, can be achieved by pruning back quite severely before new growth starts in the warmer weather, as this will encourage branching out.

Aeonium arboreum 'Schwarzkopf'

ALOCASIA SANDERIANA 'BLACK VELVET' (ELEPHANT'S EAR PLANT)

This tender perennial from the Philippines is often grown as a house plant. Although its flowers are negligible, its slightly pilose leaves (which give rise to the common name for the genus) are very eye-catching, with their distinctive black-grey with white ribbing and purple underside, upon palest green stems.

The one drawback is that all parts of this plant are extremely poisonous, so avoid it if you have young children.

The alocasia will burn in full sun, so place away from the window. Feed and water well during spring and summer, but take great care to avoid splashing the leaves when watering, as it will mark them.

GROW HOW

Size: 30–40cm (12–16in).

Season: Evergreen.

Site: Humus-rich soil. Partial to full shade.

Propagation: Cuttings/Division/Offsets.

Hardly water in winter, and don't allow the temperature to drop below 10°C (50°F).

Alocasia can be propagated by division, removing offsets from the rhizome, or by stem cuttings.

Young leaves will initially be deep green.

ALOE MITRIFORMIS

This aloe is a native of South Africa. Although, ideally, it requires sub-tropical conditions to thrive, it will tolerate being placed outside in the warmer summer months almost as successfully as the aeonium (see page 68). Its symmetrical deep red-purple rosettes, which are the colour of congealed blood, are edged with dangerous yellow thorns and can reach 30cm (1ft) in diameter. It can also produce red flowers in the right conditions.

When the aloe is indoors, it should not be subjected to a temperature below 10°C (50°F). It needs very little watering at any time, in fact the soil should be allowed to dry out completely between waterings from late spring to early autumn, and should not be watered at all during winter.

The aloe will benefit from being re-potted annually. You can propagate by taking leaf cuttings, or from offsets but, if your plant has flowered, then it can easily be grown from seed sown in March. It will require greenhouse conditions of 21°C (70°F) to achieve successful germination.

GROW HOW

Size: 60cm (2ft).

Season: Evergreen.

Site: Dry, very well-drained, gritty, loam-based soil. Full sun.

Propagation: Cuttings/Offsets/Seed.

ANTHRISCUS SYLVESTRIS (COW PARSLEY)

Anthriscus sylvestris 'Ravenswing'

This biennial is more familiar to us as an off-white umbelliferous plant of the meadow and hedgerow, but it does have dark cultivars too.

GROW HOW

Size: 1m (39in).

Season: Summer.

Site: Well-drained, but moist soil. Full sun to partial shade.

Propagation: Seed.

A Dark Selection

A. s. 'Moonlit Night'
Bronzed purple-black leaves and white umbels.

A. s. 'Ravenswing'
Purple-black leaves and off-white umbels.

Deadheading will keep the cow parsley perennial but, as an essentially wild flower, it is a prolific self-seeder and will naturalize unaided. It is best suited to an informal garden but, if you wish to control it, collect the seed in autumn and sow it in position.

BEGONIA REX CULTORUM

The begonia is another tender perennial which is often treated as either an annual or a greenhouse plant. The Rex group is certainly king when it comes to producing dark-leaved cultivars but the more common begonias – sold as summer bedding plants for their pink and white flowers – also produce bronze-leaved specimens, for instance the Malaga and Allegra strains.

GROW HOW

Size: 20–30cm (8–12in).
Season: Evergreen.
Site: Moist, rich soil. Partial to full shade.
Propagation: Cuttings.

Begonia masoniana

A Dark Selection

B. rex 'Black Knight'
Black-red with pinkish dotting.

B. rex 'Helen Lewis'
Black-purple with an inset white ring.

B. masoniana
Brown-black markings in the shape of a cross within a bright green edging.

Begonias will thrive in a humid, shady atmosphere during the warm summer months. If in pots, watering should be from the base and contact with the leaves and crown of the rhizome should be avoided. Hardly water at all in winter, and don't allow the ambient temperature to fall below 13°C (55°F).

Propagation can be undertaken by cuttings from the rhizome (although this method presents practical difficulties and the very real risk of losing your plant) or from the leaves, which is a much simpler task. A single leaf can produce several new plants, as each leaf can be cut into about four pieces horizontally across the main vein. Thus each cutting contains a part of that vein from which the new roots develop. Insert the leaf cuttings 6–12mm (¼–½in) into slightly moist compost which has been watered from beneath. Once rooted they can be re-potted into individual pots containing gritty, soil-less compost, and potted on as necessary.

BETA VULGARIS (SWISS CHARD)

Swiss chard belongs to the beet genus. It is a drought-tolerant biennial, which can be admired as an ornamental addition to a potager, or dug up and eaten – leaf and stem. The leaf colour is good all year round.

GROW HOW

Size: 45cm (18in).

Season: Summer through to the following spring, unless you eat them all.

Site: Rich, moist soil. Full sun to partial shade.

Propagation: Seed.

A Dark Selection

B. v. 'Bull's Blood'
Oozing, glossy red-black leaves on bright red stems.

B. v. 'Macgregor's Favourite'
A more purple tinge. (See picture below).

Though a biennial, Swiss chard is grown as an annual vegetable. Seed can be sown in early spring or late summer, though planting later will mean a lesser crop. Thin young seedlings to 30cm (1ft) apart, and keep well watered during hot spells. In winter, covering with straw or a polytunnel will help to ensure crop quality.

Beta vulgaris 'Macgregor's Favourite'

MARANTA LEUCONEURA (PRAYER PLANT)

Maranta leuconeura var. *erythroneura*

This low-growing, tender perennial is native to the rainforests of Brazil. The common names of the varieties provide apt descriptions of the pattern of brown-black markings on the green leaves of this small evergreen plant.

The prayer plant needs humid, warm and shady conditions which should not fall below 15°C (60°F). Re-pot annually in spring or early summer and, at the same time, propagate by division; otherwise, basal stem cuttings can be taken in summer.

A Dark Selection

M. leuconeura var. *kerchoviana*
(rabbit tracks)

M. leuconeura var. *erythroneura*
(herringbone plant)

GROW HOW

Size: 20cm (8in).

Season: Evergreen.

Site: Moist soil. Full shade.

Propagation: Cuttings/Division.

MENTHA x *PIPERITA* (BLACK PEPPERMINT)

This annual plant has an unusually dark black-purple sheen to its leaves, and the bright sunshine can intensify this colouring.

As black peppermint can be invasive, it is best grown in pots outdoors, or indoors on the windowsill.

GROW HOW

Size: 60cm (2ft).

Season: Summer.

Site: Almost anywhere.

Propagation: Seed.

A lot of herbs are sown at intervals to provide a continual supply for the kitchen, but mint is such a fast grower that a schedule of sowings is not really necessary. Pre-chill the seed, sow in early spring in trays or pots, and place in a sunny spot indoors until germination. If you are transplanting the seedlings outside, put them in containers or a self-contained herb bed to prevent their invasion of other garden space. Herbs often have better quality leaves if they are prevented from flowering and setting seed of their own accord, so it's best either to nip out the flowers before they open, or to allow some to flower, and collect the seed for sowing the following year.

Mentha x *piperita*

OCIMUM BASILICUM (BASIL)

This half-hardy annual herb has highly aromatic leaves which are used in cooking and salads (especially with tomatoes). Basil is also used as a cure for diarrhoea in some rural communities native to the Asian subcontinent.

Ocimum basilicum 'Dark Opal'

A Dark Selection

O. b. 'Purple Ruffles'
As the name suggests, a pretty ruffled edge to shiny purple-black leaves.

O. b. 'Red Rubin'
As the name implies, a redder tinge to these purple-black leaves.

O. b. 'Dark Opal'
Deep purple-black leaves.

Sow the fine seed in spring, on top of compost in trays. Keep indoors for planting out later on, or grow in pots on the windowsill. Germination can take from a week to a month. In sheltered situations, when all chance of frost has passed, seed can be sown directly outside, at a depth of 1cm (⅜in). For better quality leaves, nip flowers out before they open. Alternatively, allow some flowers to open, and collect the seed for sowing the following year.

GROW HOW

Size: 45–60cm (18–24in).

Season: Summer.

Site: Well-drained soil. Full sun.

Propagation: Seed.

OXALIS TRIANGULARIS (SORREL)

This Brazilian sorrel has delicate pinky white flowers peeking out from under deep purple trifoliate leaves. Sorrel is a good ground-cover plant, when grown outside in a sheltered site. Though this variety has generally been grown as a house plant, it is in fact tolerant of temperatures down to minus 5°C (42°F).

Sow seed in spring each year; it will only be hardy in sheltered sites, but it may survive the winter if you give it a good, dry mulch. However, it will be perennial if grown indoors in a pot, in which case you can

GROW HOW

Size: 15cm (6in).

Season: June–July for flowers. Evergreen if kept as a houseplant.

Site: Well-drained, gritty soil. Full sun.

Propagation: Cuttings/Division/Seed.

produce more stock by dividing it in early spring. Allow the surface of the soil to dry out completely between waterings.

Oxalis triangularis

PEPEROMIA GRISEOARGENTEA (IVY/SILVER LEAF PEPPER)

Peperomia griseoargentea

This is an epiphytic plant in the rainforests of Brazil, but we can see it at ground level when grown as a house plant. The cultivar called 'Nigra' has, like all peperomia, fleshy, rounded leaves, but this cultivar is particularly attractive, exhibiting crinkled, metallic black leaves which darken further near the veins. Its flowers are insignificant.

This succulent needs constant moisture, and misting of the leaves, as well as feeding during summer. It also needs moisture during winter, when the temperature should not drop below 15°C (60°F).

GROW HOW

Size: 15–20cm (6–8in).

Season: Evergreen.

Site: Rich, moist soil. Shade to indirect sunlight.

Propagation: Cuttings/Division/Seed.

Because it is a succulent, the easiest method of propagation is to take leaf or stem cuttings in spring.

PERILLA FRUTESCENS

This aromatic annual originated in China. With its 'wet-look' leaves it was a popular plant with the Victorians, and some amenity horticulturalists still use it in groups or rows to accentuate summer bedding schemes. It looks good enough to eat, and in fact is. It bears insignificant white flowers from July to August.

A Dark Selection

P. f. *atropurpurea*
Purple-red leaves.

P. f. var. *nankinensis laciniata*
Glossy bronze-purple to almost black, crinkle-edged leaves.

P. f. var. *crispa rubra*
Slightly redder leaves.

Sow seed indoors in late winter. Sow plenty, as germination – which occurs at 18°C (64°F) – is sometimes slow and not always successful. Harden off young plants before planting out in late May/early June. Pinching out will produce bushier specimens and more leaves for your salad.

Perilla frutescens var. *nankinensis*

Perilla frutescens var. *crispa rubra*

GROW HOW

Size: 60–100cm (23–40in).

Season: Summer.

Site: Well-drained, rich soil. Full sun.

Propagation: Seed.

PSEUDOPANAX FEROX (TOOTHED LANCEWOOD)

This strange, primeval, evergreen tree from New Zealand is reminiscent of a dinosaur itself, with its long, narrow, jagged-edged blades – you can hardly call them stems or leaves. The blades are a grey-black colour with a central red spine and also grey-white

GROW HOW

Size: Up to 7m (21ft).

Season: Evergreen.

Site: Fertile, well-drained soil. Sheltered site in full sun to partial shade.

Propagation: Cuttings/Seed.

slightly raised blotches along the length. This most definitely one for Des Esseintes' collection of real, yet artificial-looking plants (see Introduction, page 4).

It is best grown in containers, so that it can be brought inside during winter, when watering should be kept to a minimum. Avoid exposing it to temperatures under 10°C (50°F), although it can survive at a lower temperature.

Pseudopanax ferox can be propagated from semi-ripe cuttings taken in summer, or from seed in autumn, if you want more than one. It is a beast that will withstand hard pruning when older.

Pseudopanax ferox

SOLENOSTEMON SCUTELLARIOIDES (SYN. *COLEUS BLUMEI*)

This tender perennial from South-East Asia was at its most popular in the latter half of the nineteenth century, when new varieties were awaited with anticipation and attracted hefty prices. It's more familiar to us as a house plant but it can be used outdoors for summer bedding. It is an easy plant to propagate and maintain, and new varieties are increasing interest once again.

A Dark Selection

S. s. 'Black Prince'
A very dark example, especially the new leaf.

S. s. 'Palisandra'
This maroon-black example also has attractive pale pink flower spires.

Bicolours:
S. s. 'Black Dragon'
The leaves have an almost blood-red centre with crinkled black edging.

S. s. 'Inky Fingers'
Narrow, irregular leaves edged in a lighter reddish shade.

GROW HOW

Size: 30–60cm (1–2ft).

Season: Evergreen.

Site: Loam-enriched, moist soil. Indirect sunlight to partial shade.

Propagation: Cuttings/Seed.

Solenostemon scutellarioides

Solenostemon scutellarioides 'Inky Fingers'

Seed can be sown in late winter/early spring under glass, and will require about 16°C (61°F) to germinate. For larger annual plants, you can sow as early as January.

However, if you are not treating them as annual bedding plants and want to enjoy the colourful leaves indoors during the winter months, they will need a minimum winter temperature of 10° C (50°F).

It's best to remove the flower spires, which in most cases are an insignificant adjunct to the colourful leaves, and to propagate by taking cuttings rather than collecting seed.

Pinching out the flower stems and some of the new shoots will promote bushier growth, and you can then take tip cuttings (from non-flowering shoots) in early spring or late summer. To do this, cut just below a leaf node, and remove the lower leaves. They can be rooted in a container of water in about three weeks, as long as the surrounding air temperature is 16°C (61°F). Once roots are established, carefully plant the brittle roots in compost.

Regularly pot on according to the size of plant you want, and make sure that the plants are kept well watered and well fed throughout the summer months.

TRADESCANTIA PALLIDA
(SYN. *SETCREASEA PURPUREA*) (SPIDER LILY)

This trailing tender perennial originated in Mexico. It has a cultivar, 'Purple Heart', with narrow, dark purple-black leaves and delicate tiny pink flowers, one of which appears at the end of each stem. It looks very attractive in a hanging basket, either indoors or out.

Propagation is easy by tip or basal cuttings, or by seed. Tip cuttings can be taken at any time, except during the coldest months. Basal cuttings should be taken between May and August and, in order to produce roots, need to be planted in pots kept at a temperature of 16°C (61°F). Seed can germinate in less than a month, but to do so it must be kept in very warm – i.e. 20–27°C (68-80°F) – and dark and moist conditions. In fact the plant needs warmth all year round, but can tolerate temperatures down to 7°C (45°F). It can therefore be put outside as early as April in temperate zones.

GROW HOW

Size: 30–40cm (12–16in).

Season: Flowers May–December and evergreen if kept as a house plant.

Site: Very well-drained soil. Full, but not harsh, sun.

Propagation: Cuttings/Seed.

Tradescantia pallida 'Purple Heart'

FOLIAGE

HARDY PERENNIALS

AJUGA REPTANS (BUGLE)

Bugle is native to the Old World, but found almost everywhere. It's often used as an edging plant in municipal schemes – as a carpeting plant under larger, greedier plants – or at the front of a border. It is also good for a rockery.

Ajuga reptans 'Braunherz'

A Dark Selection

A. r. 'Atropurpurea'
30cm (1ft). Bronze-purple leaves.

A. r. 'Braunherz'
15cm (6in). Dark and glossy purple-black leaves and deep blue flower spikes.

A. r. 'Catlins Giant'
20cm (8in). Large, dark brownish-purple to green-black leaves with blue flower spikes.

A. r. 'Pink Surprise'
15cm (6in). Dark purple-black leaves and pinky-purple flower spikes.

Propagate by division, ideally in spring or late summer, or by separating and replanting the stolons. It can also be grown from seed, which should be lightly covered. It will take about one month to germinate in quite cool conditions of 10°C (50°F).

GROW HOW

Size: Various.

Season: Evergreen. (Flowers spring to summer).

Site: Almost any, but avoid hot, dry, exposed sites. Full shade to full sun.

Propagation: Division/Stolons.

CIMICIFUGA (BUGBANE)

Cimicifuga is a plant for the back of a border, not just because of its height (which means that it will need supporting canes), but also because of the slightly pungent smell. The dark-leaved varieties provide a perfect foil to the late-flowering creamy-white spires.

A Dark Selection

C. racemosa 'Purpurea'
1.5m (59in). Deep purple flushed foliage.

C. simplex var. *ramosa atropurpurea*
This is darker and taller (at 2m/79in), and includes the cultivar 'Brunette'.

GROW HOW

Size: 1.5-2m (5–6½ft).

Season: July–September.

Site: Moist, rich soil. Partial shade.

Propagation: Division/Seed.

This plant will benefit if the soil is annually enriched with leaf mould, and cut back after flowering ends in the early autumn. Germination is slow and seed should be barely covered in compost. If there is no sign of germination after three months, chill and try again. Alternatively, divide established clumps in spring.

Cimicifuga racemosa 'Purpurea'

HEUCHERA (ALUM ROOT)

A genus of evergreen, summer-flowering perennials, forming large clumps of leaves, often tinted with purple. Good ground-cover plant, especially in woodland conditions, or under deciduous hedging.

A Dark Selection

H. americana 'Palace Purple'

There are numerous other darkish-leaved heuchera, but none is as dark as the above.

Plant deep and divide every three years or so in late summer to late autumn, using young, outer portions of woody crown.

GROW HOW

Size: 60cm (2ft).

Season: Evergreen (flowers April–May).

Site: Moist soil. Full sun to partial shade.

Propagation: Division.

Heuchera americana 'Palace Purple'

LOBELIA FULGENS

Lobelia fulgens 'Queen Victoria'

This clump-forming, half-hardy perennial has cultivars that are valued both for their glossy black-red strappy leaves, which appear to glisten in the sunlight, and their spires of bright red flowers, which appear in mid- to late summer.

Divide established plants in spring. Avoid planting in ground that can become boggy, as too much wet will rot the roots; better to lift the plants and overwinter them indoors.

A Dark Selection

L. f. 'Queen Victoria'
L. f. 'Russian Princess'

GROW HOW

Size: 100cm (39½in).

Season: August–September.

Site: Well-drained soil. Full sun.

Propagation: Division.

LYSIMACHIA CILIATA (LOOSESTRIFE)

This clump-forming and summer-flowering plant is known for its dark chocolate foliage and its small yellow buttercup-like flowers. The leaf colour intensifies in the sunlight.

A Dark Selection

L. c. 'Firecracker'
L. c. 'Vesuvius'

Lysimachia needs to be kept well-watered during dry spells. It spreads fairly quickly, and established clumps will need supports in place to help them keep their shape in the border. Don't be afraid to cut back hard at the end of the season.

See also *Lysimachia atropurpurea* (under Flowers: Hardy Perennials, p. 59).

GROW HOW

Size: 100cm (39½in).

Season: Summer.

Site: Moist, even marginal, soil. Full sun to partial shade.

Propagation: Division/Seed.

Lysimachia ciliata 'Firecracker'

OPHIOPOGON PLANISCAPUS 'NIGRESCENS' (BLACK GRASS)

Ophiopogon planiscapus 'Nigrescens'

Also known as 'snake's beard' (a literal translation from the Greek), this 'grass' from Japan actually belongs to the lily family. It is a truly black plant, but also has small pale pink to violet (or sometimes white) flowers, mid- to late summer, which are followed by purple-black berries.

GROW HOW

Size: 20cm (8in).

Season: Evergreen.

Site: Fertile, well-drained, sandy soil. Full sun to partial shade in a sheltered situation.

Propagation: Division/Seed/Stolons.

It is a self-sufficient plant requiring little attention, and very versatile – it can be planted with almost anything to give a hint of blackness to your planting scheme.

O. japonicus 'Minor' is a 'miniature' variety, which has very dark green-black leaves that spread out to a mere 8cm (3in).

This plant can be grown from seed, which should be sown in autumn. A pre-soaking in cool water aids germination, although only about 60% will be true to the parent, so it is better to divide. It is slow growing, and spreads underground by means of stolons put out from the parent tuber; division of these from the parent in spring is the best way to multiply your stock.

RANUNCULUS FICARIA (LESSER CELANDINE)

The cultivar 'Brazen Hussey' has the normal little yellow flowers, but they appear above very dark olive-black shiny leaves. It is a low-growing plant, which sometimes spreads too far, but it is good under hedging or where little else will grow.

Ranunculus ficaria 'Brazen Hussey'

GROW HOW

Size: 15cm (6in).

Season: April–May.

Site: Damp, rich soil. Partial shade.

Propagation: Division/Seed.

Ranunculus can be grown from seed: sow in autumn, either in position or in a cold frame, with the seeds barely covered. But it is easier to divide established clumps in late summer to early autumn, when both flowers and foliage have died back.

SAXIFRAGA FORTUNEI (SAXIFRAGE)

It is alleged that the root of the common saxifrage will get rid of freckles and kidney stones. It tends to be thought of as a rock garden plant, but the *S. fortunei*, which originates in China and Japan, prefers a more woodland habitat. One particularly dark-leaved cultivar is 'Black Ruby', which has black leaves surmounted by tiny sprays of delicate, star-like, ruby-coloured flowers.

Another dark candidate, this time in terms of flowers, is 'Marshall Joffre' which has deep red-black buds and deep red flowers, but this quickly fades. This saxifrage prefers more alpine conditions.

GROW HOW

Size: 15–20cm (6–8in).

Season: Deciduous (Flowers October – November).

Site: Moist, neutral to acidic soil. Partial to full shade.

Propagation: Division/Seed.

Sow seed straight away when it is ripe. Alternatively, if you are storing it for a spring sowing, cold-stratify it before sowing on moist, but never wet, compost.

SEDUM (STONECROP)

Sedum telephium 'Bertram Anderson'

A Dark Selection

S. *aizoon* 'Euphorbioides'
25cm (10in). Bronze leaves and bronze flowers.

S. *telephium maximum* 'Atropurpureum'

S. *t.* 'Bertram Anderson'
15cm (6in). Slight blueberry bloom to the nearly black leaves and dark pink flowers.

S. *t.* 'Arthur Branch'
20cm (8in). Deep purple leaves and mahogany flowers.

S. *t.* 'Purple Emperor'
40cm (16in). Almost black leaves, and red flowers earlier than the others, from June.

S. t. 'Vera Jameson'
15cm (6in). Slightly iridescent quality to the purple leaves, pinkish flowers.

'Matrona', 'Mohrchen' and 'Munstead Red' are other candidates that are good specimens, but not quite as dark leaved.

The sedum is an easy plant to grow and a welcome addition to the late-flowering border, both for its leaf and its flower colour. Most of the darkest cultivars are from the *Sedum telephium* species (also known as orpine). This species requires a bit more moisture than most, but sedum generally are pretty good drought-tolerant plants, as well as being good spreaders.

GROW HOW

Size: Various.

Season: Generally evergreen. Flowers Aug. to Oct. (except 'Purple Emperor').

Site: Most soils, but well-drained. Full sun.

Propagation: Cuttings/Division.

Propagate sedum by division over the dormant winter period to early spring, but preferably when the ground is not too hard. Alternatively, take stem cuttings in spring before new growth is about to start, and up to about July, i.e. before the plant's energies are diverted to flower production.

It is possible to grow the species, but not the cultivar, from seed sown uncovered in autumn and left in the cold frame. Plant out young plants from late autumn to spring – they are frost hardy to minus 15°C (25°F).

It's not necessary to cut back the stems straight after flowering, as they look good with a winter frost on them. But, more practically, leaving the fleshy stems in position ensures that they will dry out naturally. And, cutting the stems out once they have dried, will ensure that less damage is caused to the plant.

A related plant, sempervivum (houseleek) can also come up with some dark rosettes, for example the cultivars 'Atropurpureum' and 'Nigrum'.

The houseleek was used in ointments for burns and warts, and grown on the rooftops by Celts, in the belief that it would protect their homes from lightning. It was also, in English folklore, planted outside the home to deter witches.

TRIFOLIUM REPENS 'QUADRIFOLIUM' (SCOTTISH SHAMROCK)

Trifolium repens 'Quadrifolium'

This clover is a rhizomatous, low-growing and spreading plant, that can be very invasive. However this example is quite a good-looking plant, in a small clump, with its purple-black leaves edged in green. It also comes, as 'Atropurpureum', with three leaves and with a hint of red.

GROW HOW

Size: 5cm (2in).

Season: Deciduous.

Site: Almost anywhere. Full sun.

Propagation: Don't.

TREES, SHRUBS AND GRASSES

ACER PALMATUM (JAPANESE MAPLE)

Japanese maples are beautiful in both spring and autumn and, because they are very slow-growing trees, they can be included in an otherwise herbaceous border or can be containerized.

They offer many dark purple-leaved cultivars such as *Acer platanoides* 'Crimson King' (see picture below). The others listed are particularly striking but not as easily obtainable.

A Dark Selection

A. p. 'Shojo'

Acer platanoides 'Crimson King'

A. p. '**Suminagashi**'
Bright purple-red changing to red-black. (See picture overleaf)

A. p. '**O-kagami**'
The shiniest of black-red leaves referred to by 'kagami' meaning mirror.

A. p. '**Tamukeyama**'
Dark purple-red, becoming redder in autumn.

GROW HOW

Size: 3–4m (9–12ft).

Season: Deciduous.

Site: Well-drained, moist and fertile, neutral to acidic soil. Partial shade in a sheltered situation.

Propagation: Cuttings/Grafting/Seed.

Cultivars can only be propagated by grafting, but the variety can be grown quite easily from seed. It must be cold-stratified for about two months, then sown in pots in spring, or it can be sown *in situ*, if you have a suitably sheltered site. Pot up infrequently and plant out when two to three years old, preferably in dappled shade. Water well during spring and summer.

Acer palmatum 'Suminagashi'

Obviously you need patience, because acers are so slow growing, but you could always try to grow them as bonsai. In fact an acer of any size can do well in a container in the garden, but it must be protected from full sun – which will scorch and burn the young leaves – and from winter and late frosts, which can kill. So surround your acer with a deep mulch and, if possible, cover the branches in horticultural fleece, too.

Don't forget that a well-grown tree may also need to be protected against theft, as a good specimen of Japanese maple, only 1m (39in) tall, can cost around £100 to replace and is therefore a target.

Though you may be tempted to prune and train this tree to a certain shape, why interfere with the growth of the perfect tree? Better to leave it to nature.

COPROSMA REPENS

This evergreen is native to New Zealand, and although it is a fairly low-spreading shrub initially, it can reach up to 2m (6ft) in height and spread. Like holly, the presence of male and female plants will give you red berries in the autumn.

The name coprosma is derived from *copros* – dung, but fortunately that aroma is only experienced if the leaves are crushed.

GROW HOW

Size: Up to 2m (6ft).

Season: Evergreen.

Site: Well-drained soil. Full sun.

Propagation: Cuttings/Seed.

Coprosma repens

Coprosma is hardy to 2°C (36°F), and so it can survive the winter outside if it is planted in a sheltered spot and protected by a good mulch. But if your plant is containerized, it is a good idea to bring it to a cool indoor spot to over the winter and place it outside again in the summer.

Propagate using cuttings taken between late summer and early autumn, or by sowing seed in the spring. Seed will need four to six weeks to germinate, preferably with some form of underheating to the pots. They will take two to three years to reach a reasonable size, and should then be potted on as needed in spring.

CORNUS ALBA (DOGWOOD)

There are several varieties of dogwood, but the cultivar 'Kesselringii' comes from *Cornus alba*. This is included in this selection not for its dark foliage, but for its dark blackish-purple stems. Because the dogwood is a deciduous shrub, these stems can be seen to best effect out of season.

Cornus alba 'Kesselringii'

GROW HOW

Size: Up to 2m (6ft).

Season: Deciduous.

Site: Moist, even slightly boggy, neutral to acidic soil. Full sun to almost full shade.

Propagation: Cuttings/Layerings/Suckers.

Propagate by taking heeled softwood cuttings in summer and rooting them in a 50/50 sand and peat substitute mixture; place them in a cold frame to overwinter, then pot them on in the spring.

Alternatively, pot hardwood cuttings or rooted suckers in late autumn. *C. alba* can also be propagated by layering in autumn, and the new plants detached from the parent plant a year later and potted. The young plant (two–three years old) can be planted out in either autumn or spring.

The current year's stems have the brightest colouring, and cutting back hard, literally to within a few inches of the ground in April, will encourage plenty of new growth in time for your winter display of bare branches. This can be done every year, and will help keep it under control, but it is important to feed it well after such a severe pruning. You can rest assured, however, that the dogwood is a vigorous shrub that will keep coming back for more.

CORYLUS MAXIMA 'PURPUREA' (FILBERT)

A shrub/small tree with deciduous black-purple leaves with a hint of red to them, and contrasting yellow catkins in spring which produce nuts in autumn. A very hardy specimen even in very cold climes.

GROW HOW

Size: Up to 6m x 5m (18–15ft).

Season: Deciduous.

Site: Well-drained, rich soil. Full sun to partial shade, preferably in a wind-sheltered position.

Propagation: Layering/Seed.

Layer in autumn and cut from the parent shrub after a year, when the layered stem should be adequately rooted. Pot up the young shrub regularly, for at least another year, and then plant in a suitable site anytime between October and March. Make sure the branches are no longer than 45cm (18in), so the young shrub is not overextended as it makes the transition from pot to plot.

Seed won't always be true to its parent for this species but, if you do want to attempt it, sow seed in pots in late autumn and put in a cold frame. Once germinated, treat as per layered offspring.

This filbert should be pruned annually, following a pruning manual to get the best results in terms of shape and nutting.

Corylus maxima 'Purpurea'

FAGUS SYLVATICA f. *PURPUREA* (COPPER BEECH)

Fagus sylvatica 'Purpurea Pendula'

This perhaps is the most popular and versatile dark-leaved tree native to Britain; it is adaptable to many different conditions, is often used as hedging, but also has weeping varieties. The full-sized tree can grow up to 30m (90ft) tall and many metres in diameter, but there are also smaller cultivars including, 'Dawyck Purple', 7m (21ft), and the weeping beeches 'Haaren', 6m (18ft) and 'Purpurea Pendula', 3m (9ft). A particularly black upright cultivar is *F. sylvatica* 'Riversii'.

Cultivars do not come true from seed, and require a degree of expertise to grow from grafting or budding. Do not plant out until the young tree is over two years old.

GROW HOW

Size: Up to 30m (90ft).

Season: Deciduous.

Site: Almost all soils, except waterlogged. Full sun.

Propagation: Grafting/Budding.

If you are growing it for hedging, the first pruning should be in late summer, when the plants are over three years old. However, if you are growing a weeping version of the beech, resist the urge to prune, unless it is to remove dead or broken branches.

MAGNOLIA LILIIFLORA 'NIGRA'
(SYN. MAGNOLIA x SOULANGEANA 'NIGRA')

This magnolia from China is not included for its leaves but for its beautiful, yet fleeting and easily damaged, dark purple upright flowers, which have dark purple veining on their lighter coloured interiors.

GROW HOW

Size: Up to 4m (12ft).

Season: April–June.

Site: Well-drained, rich, neutral to acidic soil. Full sun in a sheltered situation.

Propagation: Cuttings/Layering.

Magnolia can be grown from heel cuttings, which should be taken in July and placed in a gritty mixture in a warm propagator, 21°C (70°F) to root. It can also be grown by layering, but it is a slow-growing specimen, and would take about two years to root.

Pruning should not be necessary beyond removing dead or broken branches, and this should be done after flowering.

Magnolia liliiflora 'Nigra'

MELICA ALTISSIMA 'ATROPURPUREA'

This clump-forming, evergreen grass produces a profusion of 10cm (4in) spikes of dark brown flowers which bob in the breeze on drooping stems.

Other grasses with dark flowers/seedheads include the smaller *Carex stricta* 'Aurea', which has black seedheads symmetrically dotted with green, that briefly contrast with the bright green leaves; and setaria, which has dark flower spikes.

The melica seed will germinate within the month, or in up to three months if kept at a relatively low temperature of 10° C (50°F).

GROW HOW

Size: Up to 90cm. (3ft)

Season: Evergreen (flowers May–August).

Site: Moist, alkaline soil. Full sun to full shade.

Propagation: Seed.

The seed is minute so, if collected rather than left to naturalize, sow it at once *in situ* and barely cover. Grasses are tough and can be pretty much left to their own devices.

PAEONIA DELAVAYI 'FRANCH.' (TREE PEONY)

Paeonia suffruticosa 'Sumi-no-ichi'

The tree peony was the subject of a mania in China similar to that experienced by the tulip in Holland nearly a thousand years later (see 'A Potted Introduction', p.4). The flower has especial significance to both the Chinese, for whom it is a signifier of spring, and to the Japanese – who are today its most prolific breeders – as a signifier of prosperity. Along with the cherry blossom and lotus it is one of the flowers of royalty and, for this reason, should not be displayed in vases with any other blooms.

P. delavayi 'Franch.' is native to western China, and was named after Franchet, the nineteenth century plantsman who brought it into Europe. It has exceptionally dark brown-black single flowers, which are black in bud, and in full bloom have a hint of black-red and red-orange stamens. The serrated leaves and new shoots have a purple tinge. This variety is a particularly good source for hybrids and cultivars, which, unless otherwise stated, are in shades of black-red and have single blooms.

A Dark Selection

P. d. 'Fuyugarasu'

P. d. 'Kokko-no-tsukasa' (Black Leader)
Black-red with white stripes.

P. d. 'Kokko-shi' (King of Black Light)
P. d. 'Koku-ho' (Black Bird)
P. d. 'Koku-tsuru' (Black Crane)

P. d. 'Ruriban'
Black-purple with yellow centre.

P. d. 'Shunkodin' (Temple of Good Fortune)
Black-purple double.

P. d. 'Sumi-no-ichi' (Deepest Ink)
Maroon-black.

P. d. 'Sumina-gashi' (Dark Streak)
Black-red with white stripes.

There are also the USA Saunders hybrids, mostly bred in 1948, which bloom slightly later, including, 'Black Douglas' a double, 'Black Panther' a semi-double, and 'Black Pirate', 'Corsair', 'Heart of Darkness', 'Monitor' and 'Thunderbolt'. Also *P. lactiflora* 'Chocolate Soldier'.

Like camellias, tree peonies should be planted in a situation that avoids the harsh early morning sun and in soil that is enriched annually with bonemeal and manure. Though they like a moist soil, it should have good drainage, as this will

GROW HOW
Size: Up to 1.5m (59in).
Season: March–May.
Site: Well-drained, moist, alkaline to neutral soil. Full sun to partial shade.
Propagation: Division/Grafting/Layering/Seed/Suckers.

minimize the chance of it catching its characteristic mould or wilt.

Propagation is only for the experienced gardener, and grafting is the most successful method. It is possible to create new plants by division in autumn, but great care should be taken as they don't like root disturbance. It is preferable to use suckers or layering but, with the latter method, it will take at least a couple of years to root, before producing a new plant.

Unfortunately, cuttings, which should be taken in late autumn, do not have a high success rate and cultivars do not come true from seed. The variety's seed can be sown in autumn, but it will not flower for at least five years, and it must not be planted out until four years old.

Pot on and keep in the cold frame over winter, and place outdoors in the summer.

You should not need to prune the tree peony, except to clear out the dead wood.

PHORMIUM TENAX 'PURPUREUM' (NEW ZEALAND FLAX)

This large architectural plant can survive outdoors in more sheltered sites, even in Britain.

Cordyline australis 'Purpurea' is a smaller, but less dark and less hardy alternative.

The variety, but not the cultivar, can be grown from seed. Seed should be sown in a sandy mixture in early spring, and placed in the greenhouse; germination will occur at a temperature of 15–18°C (60–65°F). It should remain containerised during its first year and only be put outside in summer.

Alternatively, you can divide the phormium in April but, once the plant has become established, this can be a difficult task.

After the first year the plant can remain outside as, despite its tropical appearance, it is able to survive in most gardens if planted out permanently. It will survive the winter – unless your garden is particularly exposed – but you must ensure that it has a protective dry mulch of leaf mould and/or bracken.

GROW HOW

Size: 3m (9ft).

Season: Evergreen.

Site: Moist, but well-drained soil. Full sun in a sheltered situation.

Propagation: Division (if you can).

PHYLLOSTACHYS NIGRA (BLACK BAMBOO)

Like *Cornus alba* 'Kesselringii' (see page 96), this bamboo has been included for its stems rather than its foliage. Native to both China and Japan, it is hardy with narrow, delicate green leaves around black stems, or more correctly culms, which are in fact green in their first year of growth.

A Dark Selection

P. n. 'Megurochiku'
Yellow-green canes with black stripes.

P. n. 'Munro'
Bushier with smaller leaves.

P. n. 'Othello'
Black culms

Another dark candidate for the garden is the fountain bamboo (*Fargesia nitida* syn. *Sinarundinaria nitida*/*Arundinaria nitida*), with culms more purple than black, which grows to a more compact size.

To produce seed, the bamboo needs to flower and, as this rarely occurs, this is an unlikely method of propagation. The old adage that a flowering bamboo will die has some basis in fact, as the energy required to produce blooms and subsequent seed seriously drains the vigour of the plant.

Instead, divide in spring, when new roots have just started to grow. Too late, and the newly divided plants will fail to establish.

With established clumps, rather than trying to lift the whole plant, it is possible – and indeed easier for you and the plant – to separate sections from its outermost edges. You will need only a small amount of above-ground growth: a few stems which are at least two years old and which have new shoots emerging nearby.

Dig out and cut off 30cm (1ft) sections, trim the culms to about 30cm (1ft) height, and pot them deeply into good, moist compost; cover, and place in a warm, light area. The root system of these sections will be sufficiently established in about one month's time for planting in their new location, either in the garden or in a container.

Containers need to be kept very well-watered. If planting in the ground, keep an eye on the spread of the plant, as it is vigorous and could get out of control.

There is no need to prune black bamboo.

GROW HOW

Size: Up to 10m (30ft), but more likely to 5m (15ft).

Season: Deciduous.

Site: Any moist soil. Full sun to partial shade.

Propagation: Cuttings/Division.

PITTOSPORUM TENUIFOLIUM

This evergreen shrub from New Zealand has as near to black leaves as you can get, though new growth is actually pale green, which can give the plant a somewhat odd appearance during its growing season. If grown as a tree it can reach up to 10m (30ft), but there are smaller cultivars available, such as the popular 'Tom Thumb'. It is a compact, densely leaved shrub, which makes it a good topiary subject. It can also be used as hedging. Its small umbelliferous flowers are purple-brown with a hint of vanilla.

The seed of pittosporum has a sticky coating; for successful germination this must be removed before sowing, so put the seeds in some dry sand and gently agitate them before sowing. In March, sow the seed in small pots and put in a cold frame.

The young plant should spend two years in a pot before being planted out in early

GROW HOW

Size: Up to 10m (30ft).
Season: Evergreen.
Site: Well-drained soil. Full sun in a sheltered situation.
Propagation: Cuttings/Seed.

summer. Basal cuttings can also be taken at this time, then brought on in greenhouse conditions of around 15°C (60°F) over winter, and planted out in late spring.

Pittosporum is slightly susceptible to cold wet winters, and benefits from a dry mulch.

Prune this shrub twice yearly: if leaves are affected by frost, remove them with quite a vigorous pruning in early spring, then prune again in late summer.

Pittosporum tenuifolium 'Tom Thumb'

PRUNUS CERASIFERA 'NIGRA' (CHERRY PLUM)

Prunus cerasifera 'Nigra' (close up)

If you attempt to grow this from seed, it may not come true but, if you wish to try, the seed needs a long period of chilling before sowing. It would be better to take heel cuttings in summer, and plant in a 50/50 mixture of sand and peat substitute, or take softwood cuttings in spring.

Cherry trees shouldn't need pruning but, if you do find it is necessary – for example to remove damaged or infected branches – this is best done in the dry heat of summer, as this will reduce the risk of fungal infections such as silver-leaf disease.

Cherry trees have been long revered and cultivated by the Japanese for their profuse yet delicate blooms which appear in early spring. There are several cherry trees that have dark red to purple leaves, particularly as autumn approaches, but *P. cerasifera* 'Nigra' has that glossy purple-black foliage from the outset.

GROW HOW

Size: Up to 10m (30ft).

Season: Deciduous. (Flowers March–April.)

Site: Well-drained soil. Full sun.

Propagation: Cuttings/Seed.

Prunus cerasifera 'Nigra'

SAMBUCUS NIGRA (BLACK ELDER)

This European tree is associated with a great deal of old English lore and superstition, mostly with witchcraft and the devil, and this found its way to America with the early settlers. Depending on the area of Britain, it was said to keep evil from your home or your loved ones' graves if planted round them as a barrier, or to encourage an unwelcome visit by the devil into your home if you burnt it on the hearth, or even just brought a twig indoors; it was never used in shipbuilding for these reasons. Witches were believed to turn into elders to avoid detection, and anyone cutting down an elder had to recite an incantation to protect himself.

GROW HOW

Size: Up to 5m (16ft).
Season: Deciduous. (Flowers June.)
Site: Any soil. Full sun.
Propagation: Cuttings.

A Dark Selection

S. n. 'Black Beauty'
Now the darkest black-purple available, with pink flowers.

S. n. 'Guincho Purple'
Previously the darkest available, with pink flowers.

S. n. 'Thundercloud'
Black-red leaves and darker pink flowers.

Although the elder will tolerate being planted in practically any situation, from heavy soil to exposed sites, the iridescent leaves look best in full sun, in spring, and tend to fade with age.

Propagate by taking semi-ripe heel cuttings in late summer and potting in a sandy mixture for drainage. Place under cover in a cold frame, then transfer to a nursery bed in spring, and plant out in the following autumn before the ground gets too hard. Prune as necessary.

Sambucus nigra

USING DARK PLANTS

INTRODUCTION

The use of dark plants in general, and black plants in particular, has found little creative outlet either in public or private schemes. The most popular combination is perhaps the most predictable, that of black with red, which features in strong planting schemes at the National Trust properties in central England of both Hidcote Manor Garden (Gloucestershire) and Coughton Court (Warwickshire).

That this combination undoubtedly works well is demonstrated by a relatively new border scheme at Coughton which combines the ubiquitous black grass *(Ophiopogon planiscapus* 'Nigrescens') with other attractions such as dark red potentillas, the *Sedum* 'Vera Jameson', the dark red *Dahlia* 'Bishop of Llandaff' (which also has dark bronze foliage), and *Aeonium arboreum* 'Schwarzkopf'.

Aeonium arboreum 'Schwarzkopf'

Ophiopogon planiscapus 'Nigrescens'

But black and red is an easy option and, while it can look stunning, there are so many other ways of using black in the garden, other than just resorting to the nearest pot of black grass; its current fashion, though, does mean that it is one of the few true black plants that is readily available, as well as easy to care for. Another is the tulip, and swathes of traditionally shaped, shining black tulips combine with the red at Hidcote, where they also plant them in a more sophisticated combination of black and white behind low box hedging. But, monochromatic schemes are loved by some and hated by the easily bored, even when combined with pleasing shades of lime green.

But why stop there? Dark plants can be combined with ivory or sherbet lemon, with pastel pinks and blues, with silvers, with golden yellows and vibrant oranges and reds, or with brooding purples and luscious greens. Ultimately, why not progress to a border or entire garden in just black – in all its subtle shades, to compete with that ghostly, all-white garden created by Vita Sackville-West at Sissinghurst, in Kent?

The easiest course to adopt when planting dark plants is to start by planting a two-colour scheme, either in a pot, hanging basket or in a small corner. The pansy and violet are among the most accessible plants to combine in any of those situations, as they are versatile enough to be left to intermingle and draw together a natural planting scheme, or to be planted minimally, on their own in a white container.

I hope that the following planting schemes will show that using dark plants won't banish all colour – vibrant or pastel – from the garden landscape, but that they can be incorporated as contrasting or complementary accents into recognisable schemes, throughout the seasons.

Cosmos astrosanguineus

DESIGN 1

WINTER TO SPRING

At this time of year there is very little going on in the garden, so with this simple design the focus is on the branches of the dogwood (cornus) – which I've made the central feature – and the foliage of the grasses.

Use the dogwood *Cornus alba* 'Kesselringii' for its deep purple stems, or *C. alba* 'Elegantissima' for burgundy-red stems, which become covered with variegated foliage in summer. In either case, to enjoy the dogwood's impressive winter colour it's important to place it in a position which, as well as being moisture retentive, will show its branches – which can reach 6–7ft (2m) in height – to best effect. My design shows an island bed with a pale gravel, shingle or bark mulch covering, which can be either circular or ovoid. This obviously requires some space but if this is limited the design could be adapted to a semi-circular bed with a suitable contrasting solid backdrop, such as evergreen hedging.

Helleborus orientalis

You could also use outdoor uplighting, which would further enhance the glow of the dogwood branches and the contrasting blue-grey and bronze colours of the surrounding grasses. All these clump-forming grasses, after losing their crown of winter frost, become brighter in the spring sunshine and produce flowers in summer; they vary in spread from 60 x 60cm (2 x 2ft) to 30 x 30cm (1 x 1ft), and in the case of the black grass a smaller 20 x 20cm (8 x 8in).

An added bonus is that the black grass (*Ophiopogon planiscapus*) – which, incidentally, is not a grass at all but a member of the lily genus – produces small mauve flowers, followed by black berries in autumn. The flowering stems increase the height and presence of the grasses to compete with the dominant feature of the dogwood in leaf. Indeed, the whole appearance of the feature 'greens' during the summer months with the foliage of the hellebores and irises, and the reversion to green of the conifer *Chamaecyparis thyoides* 'Purple Heather'.

Planting hellebores, irises, snowdrops and crocuses is optional, as not everyone will feel the need to include any flowering plants in this essentially foliate design. However, I think that there is nothing more uplifting than the first flowers of spring, so I have included late winter/early spring-flowering snowdrops and small-flowered purple-flushed crocuses. These will, eventually, give a more naturalistic appearance, softening the contrived placement of the three surrounding groups of plants; once flowering is over,

Cornus alba 'Kesselringii'

however, they will leave little trace. In fact, all the flowering plants have been chosen for their transitory nature.

Once the dogwood comes into leaf, it will hide the foliage of the hellebores underneath. However, a word of caution: planting the creamy-white Christmas rose *(Helleborus niger)* and the contrasting dark (either deep purple or slate-black hybrid) *Helleborus orientalis* is not advisable if there are young children at home, as all parts of this plant are poisonous.

No such fears with the iris. If you have the right soil conditions and want to include this optional addition to the design, you could use, 'Swazi Princess' which grows to a 90 x 60cm (3 x 2ft) clump and flowers mid-season (i.e. from early to mid June). It will not look out of place amongst the vertical shapes of the grasses, conifer and dogwood. Moreover, as the iris's tall sword-like leaves should be cut down to a third of their height at the end of the season, their presence will not detract from the minimalism of the design. (If you prefer, use an alternative shorter black/nearly black Intermediate Iris for a less dominant impact.) In fact, the crowns of the rhizomes should do well slightly exposed among the gravel/shingle surface, as the stones will retain the heat of the sun. This 'baking' effect will encourage good blooms to continue the floral accent, once the early spring-flowering bulbs have finished.

WINTER TO SPRING

1. Dogwood, *Cornus alba* 'Kesselringii' or 'Elegantissima'

2. Conifer, *Chamaecyparis thyoides* 'Purple Heather'

3. Blue fescue grass, *Festuca glauca*, e.g. 'Elijah Blue'

4. Blue oat grass, *Helictotrichon sempervirens* (syn. *Avena candida*)

5. Sedge, *Carex comans*, bronze form

6. Black grass, *Ophiopogon planiscapus* 'Nigrescens'

7. Christmas rose, *Helleborus niger* (optional)

8. *Helleborus orientalis* (optional)

9. Snowdrop, *Galanthus nivalis* (optional)

10. *Crocus chrysanthus* e.g. 'Prince Claus' or 'Ladykiller' (optional)

11. Bearded Iris, e.g. 'Swazi Princess', or 'Black Knight' (optional)

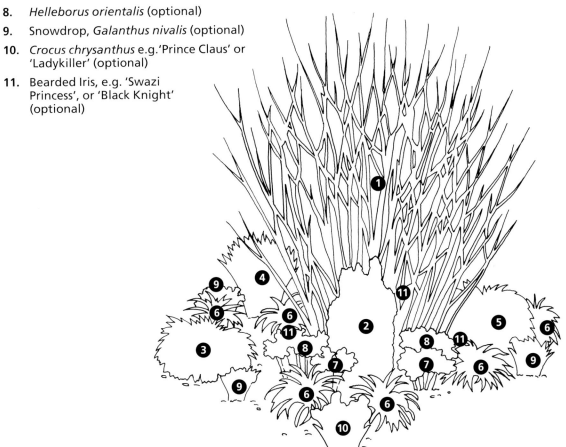

DESIGN 2

SPRING TO EARLY SUMMER

This border, suitable for any sunny secluded spot, contains a small selection of plants. Their period of flowering will fill the hiatus between spring bulbs and summer planting in a perhaps less traditional colour scheme of mahogany, with undertones of red and contrasting creamy-white shades.

The border includes a smattering of chocolate-brown, which appears as blocks of colour to the back of the border with the Grecian foxgloves, and as a flush on the petals of the pot marigold *Calendula* 'Coffee Cream' in the foreground.

Brown in its various hues is, in my opinion, a sophisticated colour in the garden. I was tempted to create a confection of plant names by including chocolate cosmos alongside 'Coffee Cream' and another pot marigold, 'French Vanilla'; not just because of the flavours that their names conjure up, but because the deep maroon/brown petals of the cosmos, as its name implies, give off such a mouth-watering, and still surprising, aroma of chocolate. I was

Delphinium 'Basil Clitheroe'

also tempted by the chocolate-flushed white flowers of the sweet pea 'Wiltshire Ripple'. But stomach-led cravings aside, this is a design intended for a small border which contains plants of some dimension and height in their maturity, and which therefore need to be few in number so that they can have adequate space to flourish. These plants can easily be left to go their own way, self-seed and then further intermingle, and there is therefore no focal point as such. But it may be advisable to keep the plants under control, if you don't want to lose the overall balance of the design.

The plants in this border are divided into two tiers, one between 90–120cm (3–4ft) tall, the other between 30–60cm (1–2ft). To the rear, the Grecian foxglove, *Digitalis lanata*, which grows to a height of approximately 90cm (3ft), is not as imposing or invasive as its English counterpart, which figures in the following design for a cottage-style border. The brown spires of the Grecian foxglove are intermingled with both those of the taller *Delphinium* 'Magic Fountains White' and the 90cm (3ft) tall *Scabiosa* 'Black Widow' in the foreground; this has, in turn, its pin-prick white stamens complemented by its slightly shorter relative, *Scabiosa* 'White Perfection'.

The double peony-like *Papaver* 'Black Beauty' is positioned slightly off-centre. Its tendency to spread or fall open in the centre will be easily masked by the surrounding planting, so that its blooms, rather than its foliage (which I admit I don't find particularly attractive), remain the focus of attention. The simple shape of the poppy flower is a foil to the sophistication of the Bearded iris, 'Provencal', to the rear left, whose upright blade-like leaves mirror the foxglove and delphinium spires to the right. Possible alternatives to 'Provencal' might be the brown-flushed iris 'Sagar Cedric', or 'Autumn Leaves'.

The lower tier at the front comprises the 45cm (18in) dark red spikes of the snapdragon 'Black Prince' above its bronze-tinted foliage, and the complementary spreading, darkly red-black fragrant blooms of the 30–40cm (12–15in) tall sweet william; this in turn contrasts with the neighbouring 45–60cm (18–24in) tall pot marigold 'French Vanilla' with its pompom blooms, and the adjacent, more daisy-like blooms on the slightly shorter *Calendula* 'Coffee Cream'. The dark centres of 'Coffee Cream' tie in with the mahogany shades in the rest of the scheme, its coffee-tinged petals adding a touch of subtlety.

SPRING TO EARLY SUMMER

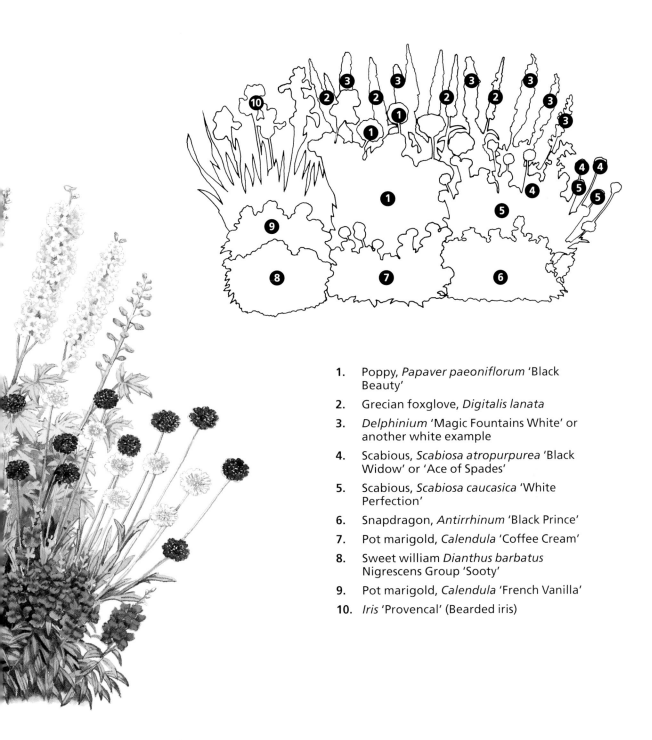

1. Poppy, *Papaver paeoniflorum* 'Black Beauty'

2. Grecian foxglove, *Digitalis lanata*

3. *Delphinium* 'Magic Fountains White' or another white example

4. Scabious, *Scabiosa atropurpurea* 'Black Widow' or 'Ace of Spades'

5. Scabious, *Scabiosa caucasica* 'White Perfection'

6. Snapdragon, *Antirrhinum* 'Black Prince'

7. Pot marigold, *Calendula* 'Coffee Cream'

8. Sweet william *Dianthus barbatus* Nigrescens Group 'Sooty'

9. Pot marigold, *Calendula* 'French Vanilla'

10. *Iris* 'Provencal' (Bearded iris)

DESIGN 3

HEIGHT OF SUMMER

This cottage-style border can be left to its own devices to a far greater extent than the previous design, even though it's a more ambitious scheme, containing over 25 different plants, and is intended for a much larger space. The dimensions are flexible, so it can either be a feature at the far end of a larger garden – as one of a series of 'rooms' currently in vogue in garden design – or it can be the predominant space, placed either facing the house or at a

Viola 'Molly Sanderson'

right angle to it. If placed at a right angle, it could be faced with a mirror image of the design on the opposite side.

Alternatively, it could face an ornamental vegetable patch; this could be intermingled with splashes of colour from Californian poppies, marigolds and other companion plants to deter pests, which would give it the feel of a potager. There are lots of especially cultivated dark vegetables that you could grow

there, to complement the black pods of the dwarf French bean 'Purple Queen' incorporated in the main design. Fortunately these vegetables and fruits turn into more palatable dark greens or deep reds on cooking! To continue the dark theme, I have used the purple beech, *Fagus sylvatica*, as hedging but this isn't strictly necessary.

The essence of such a border should be one of abundance and bio-diversity: crammed full of traditional perennials and annuals attracting a large variety of wildlife, with not a clod of earth in view, and preferably no lawn. In fact, the only 'lawn' to feature here is that directly in front of the garden seat, made of a patchwork of low-growing herbs and brick paving. The centre-piece is one of the darkest basils, *Ocimum basilicum* 'Red Rubin', which is surrounded symmetrically by beds of camomile, thyme and basil (or you could use sage). The herb beds are planted between brown bricks, so that the herbs can be picked and used, rather than crushed beneath your feet, when approaching the seat.

A cottage-style garden needs the sense of seclusion achieved by using tall plants. In this case I've used biennials: the common foxglove both in white and in its range of pinky-purples on the one side, and hollyhocks on the other. My choice of hollyhocks is the double-flowered 'Double Moonlight' and the single-flowered, dark, glossy 'Arabian Nights', but you may wish to use the slightly less dark double-flowered version of 'Arabian Nights'.

The element of height is continued into the middle ground by the use of 2m (6ft) high cane 'wigwams' to support, on the left-facing side, the delicate creamy-white sweet pea, 'Mrs Collier' whose colour complements those of the hollyhocks and the 120cm (4ft) false indigo, and on the right-facing side, the dwarf French bean, whose produce adds an unusual edible element to the dark plants in this scheme. In fact, this element is continued in the beds of 60cm (2ft) tall perilla, which can be used in salads; these emanate from the wigwam structures on both sides, bringing some unity to the planting.

The unification of the plot is also developed by duplicating the planting on either side of the garden seat and herb bed. The seat is flanked by containers on columns, which overflow with the mini trailing – and profusely pink flowering – 'Fairy' rose; this in turn is underplanted with the deep black violet 'Midnight Runner', or 'Molly Sanderson'. In front, at ground level, there are terracotta containers planted with the trailing rosemary 'Capri'. In the ground, and flanking the herbs, is a white lavender, 'Edelweiss' (an

Ocimum basilicum 'Red Rubin'

alternative might be the Dutch *Lavandula vera nana alba*), which continues the fragrant and healing herbal feel to this seated area.

The bulk of the planting area is taken up with plants which will easily spread, such as the pale fluffy pink meadow rue and dark pink, black-eyed *Geranium psilostemon* to the right, and the purple-blues of *Verbena bonariensis* and *Campanula alliarifolia* to the left. It would be a good idea also to add other cottage-style

favourites such as penstemons and columbines to extend the flowering season.

The area is edged with lower-growing black and white carnations, chocolate cosmos and the darkest cornflower I could find, *Centaurea dianthus* 'Black Ball'. Along the front is the white carnation 'Mrs Sinkins', which encloses the space, and this is partially underplanted with low-growing nemophila and violets, to soften the edge and overflow on to the path.

HEIGHT OF SUMMER

1. Purple beech, *Fagus sylvatica* f. *purpurea*
2. Mini trailing rose, 'The Fairy'
3. Violet, *Viola cornuta* 'Midnight Runner' or 'Molly Sanderson'
4. Rosemary, *Rosmarinus lavandulaceus*, 'Capri'
5. Black peppermint, *Mentha* x *piperita*
6. Red basil, e.g. 'Red Rubin', *Ocimum basilicum*
7. Camomile, *Chamaemelum nobile*
8. Basil 'Siam Queen' or sage
9. Thyme
10. Sweet pea, *Lathyrus* 'Mrs Collier'
11. Dwarf French bean 'Purple Queen' or 'Purple Teepee'
12. Hollyhock, *Alcea nigra* 'Arabian Nights'
13. Hollyhock, *Alcea* 'Double Moonlight'
14. False indigo, *Baptisia australis*
15. Foxglove, *Digitalis purpurea* (wide choice available in shades of pink)
16. Foxglove, *Digitalis purpurpea* 'Alba'
17. *Perilla frutescens* var. *nankinensis*
18. Meadow rue, *Thalictrum aquilegiafolium*
19. *Geranium psilostemon*

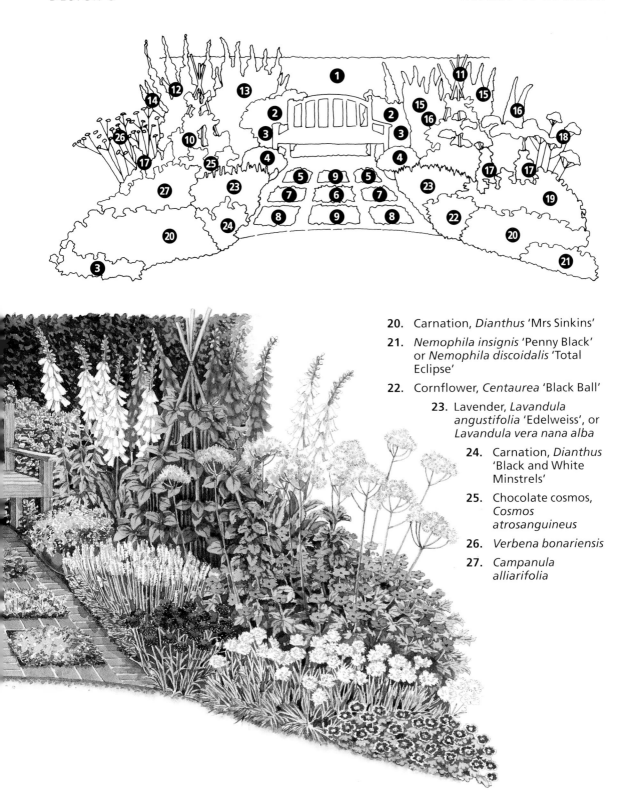

20. Carnation, *Dianthus* 'Mrs Sinkins'
21. *Nemophila insignis* 'Penny Black' or *Nemophila discoidalis* 'Total Eclipse'
22. Cornflower, *Centaurea* 'Black Ball'
23. Lavender, *Lavandula angustifolia* 'Edelweiss', or *Lavandula vera nana alba*
24. Carnation, *Dianthus* 'Black and White Minstrels'
25. Chocolate cosmos, *Cosmos atrosanguineus*
26. *Verbena bonariensis*
27. *Campanula alliarifolia*

DESIGN 4

SUMMER TO AUTUMN

Like the preceding design, this is for a large border, but in contrast it requires a lot of care and patience to achieve the magnificent vibrant late-summer display illustrated. These plants like their feet in nutrient-rich soil and their heads in the sun. Apart from regular watering, several of the plants require staking during flowering, particularly as many are profuse in blooms and tall – some up to as much as 180cm (6ft). This, of course, includes the sunflower *Helianthus* 'Chianti' (another readily available and similar variety is 'Velvet Queen') and the rudbeckias 'Green Wizard' and 'Herbstsonne'. Additionally, the dahlias 'Daytona' and 'Bishop of Llandaff' and, depending on the extent of shelter afforded by your garden, possibly the taller daylily 'Root Beer' and the coneflower 'White Swan' will also need staking.

But your work does not stop there. Unfortunately dahlia tubers, canna rhizomes and montbretia corms are not able to withstand the cold months of winter, and will need to be dug up and overwintered, by storing in dry soil in pots indoors, during their dormant months. Ideally the cabbage palms should also be brought indoors to a cool porch or greenhouse.

What is noticeably different about this border scheme is the feeling of maturity which is provided not only by these large plants, but also by the inclusion of greater structure in the form of small trees: a columnar juniper and spreading Japanese maples – the dark purple-red and a lime-green filigree-leaved *Acer palmatum*. If you wish, you could substitute a filigree-style elder, such as *Sambucus* 'Notcutt's Variety', which is named after the originating plant nursery situated close to St Albans in Hertfordshire.

Bells of Ireland (*Moluccella laevis*)

Edging the whole border with the darkest bugle, *Ajuga reptans* 'Atropurpurea', provides a containment to the exuberance of the contents of the border itself. The bugle plants wind their way around the volute-shaped ends and along the convex curve of the border, and are themselves bordered by pale slabs which act as a contrasting foil. You may not want to go to the trouble of creating the volute-shaped end sections of the border, where the terracotta pots containing specimens of dark *Cordyline australis* 'Atropurpurea' are situated. If that is the case, then place the cordylines, in their containers for ease of removal, into the main border itself. The bugle's spreading nature means that, if you want, it will eventually break up the hard edging.

An added attraction of using this bugle is that its blue flowers, while breaking with the colour scheme of blacks, greens, reds and oranges, will contrast well with the smaller than average 60cm (2ft) montbretia, *Crocosmia* 'Emily McKenzie', and the 40cm (15in) tall *Venidio* 'Tangerine', with its pale peach daisy-like flowers, which tone down the louder orange of the *Dahlia* 'Daytona' behind. But it is *Dahlia* 'Bishop of Llandaff', with its deep red blooms on black stems, that has the most striking appearance, here partially tamed by the surrounding greens of the maple (or elder) and juniper. There are several orange-flowered dahlias which have dark brown-black foliage, one of the most striking being 'Ellen Houston' which, space permitting, could also be included in this area.

To the rear the 120cm (4ft) *Canna* 'Liberation' continues the dark red/bronze-black theme. I've chosen this particular plant

Ajuga reptans 'Atropurpurea'

for its connection with the names of the daylilies – 'Root Beer' and 'America' – to their left. After all, many of the best modern cultivars of hemerocallis originate in the USA .

I've already mentioned that greens have been used to tone down the 'hot' colours in this scheme. But greens are not there just as an accent, as on the left-facing side they are given their own space. Here the green-flowering version of red hot poker – 'Percy's Pride'– nestles behind the bells of Ireland, another spire-like plant 30cm (1ft) shorter. You could also add another lower tier in front by using *Eucomis bicolor*, also known as the pineapple flower; this is 30cm (1ft) tall and has a similar appearance to 'Percy's Pride', but with an added touch of tropical exotica along the same lines as the cordyline. Lastly, the *Rudbeckia* 'Green Wizard', which is strictly speaking a black plant as the green petals are in fact sepals, acts as backdrop to the rear left and partially screens the dark sunflowers.

SUMMER TO AUTUMN

1. *Cordyline australis* 'Atropurpurea'
2. Bugle, *Ajuga reptans* 'Atropurpurea'
3. Bells of Ireland, *Moluccella laevis*
4. Red hot poker, *Kniphofia* 'Percy's Pride'
5. *Rudbeckia* 'Green Wizard'
6. Sunflower, *Helianthus* 'Chianti'
7. Juniper
8. *Montbretia* syn. *Crocosmia* x *crocosmiiflora* 'Emily McKenzie'
9. Dark purple-red Japanese maple, *Acer palmatum*
10. *Dahlia* 'Daytona'
11. *Dahlia* 'Bishop of Llandaff'

12. South African sunshine flower, *Venidio* 'Tangerine'

13. *Rudbeckia* 'Herbstsonne'

14. *Canna* 'Liberation'

15. Lime-green Japanese maple, *Acer palmatum*, or elder, *Sambucus* 'Notcutt's Variety'

16. Coneflower, *Echinacea purpurea* 'White Swan'

17. Daylily, *Hemerocallis* 'Root Beer'

18. Daylily *Hemerocallis* 'America'

DESIGN 5

SUN LOVERS

This border, in black, silver and yellow, contains plants that thrive in a sunny position, and the silver-leafed plants have a particular tolerance of dry conditions. It is perhaps the most upright of the six, in that it has three regimental groups of 60–75cm (24–30in) tall, deepest black tulips, which are backed by the equally upright 90cm (3ft) golden yellow *Eremurus* (foxtail lilies). The papery bonnets of *Aquilegia* 'Black Barlow', which bow and curtsy in the breeze on 90cm (3ft) stems, soften the formality.

These plants overlook the lower rounded forms of the similarly sized (approximately 45cm (15in), silver-foliated *Cineraria maritima* 'Silver Dust' and *Helichrysum italicum* subsp. *serotinum* which, as its common name 'curry plant' suggests, gives off a distinct, and for me nostalgic, whiff of curry powder when crushed between the fingers. To the left-facing, and continuing the silver theme, is the profusely prickly flowered and silver-blue sea holly, *Eryngium variifolium*, which as an added bonus has subtlely variegated leaves.

A central but small splash of colour in this silver lining is provided by the low-growing bi-colour pansy, *V.* x *wittrockiana* 'Brunig', whose bright yellow and black faces tie in with the yellows of the foxtail lilies and the tiny flowers of the curry plant, when it is in bloom. Another yellow, in the form of the 15cm (6in) tall pale pastel poppy *Papaver* 'Pacino', is partially hidden behind the vibrant pansy, but its delicate colour is highlighted beautifully by the backdrop of *Cineraria maritima*.

Cineraria maritima 'Silver Dust'

1. Foxtail lily, *Eremurus stenophyllus*
2. Tulip, 'Queen of Night' or 'Black Swan'
3. Columbine, *Aquilegia* 'Black Barlow'
4. *Cineraria maritima* (a.k.a. *Senecio maritima*) 'Silver Dust', or use *Artemisia* 'Powis Castle'
5. Sea holly, *Eryngium variifolium*
6. Poppy, *Papaver miyabeanum* 'Pacino'
7. Pansy, *V.* x *wittrockiana* 'Brunig'
8. Curry plant, *Helichrysum italicum* subsp. *serotinum*

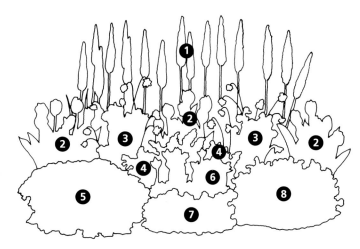

DESIGN 6

SHADE LOVERS

The plants placed in this shady spot prefer moist, humus-rich conditions, and can cope with either dappled or complete shade. Here I have deliberately included plants with appearances as well as names that conjure up a dark theme, not only to the eye but also to the psyche.

This theme is epitomized by the inclusion of two 60–75cm (24–30in) tall *Tacca chantrieri*, whose sinister bat-like features (which explain its common name) peer above 30cm (1ft) dangling fronds from behind the variegated Solomon's seal and *Hosta* 'White Christmas' on the left-facing side. Although there is something strangely fascinating about this plant and its white brother, *Tacca chantrieri alba*, if you are an arachnophobe or of nervous disposition I wouldn't blame you if you decided to leave this plant out of the scheme!

However, it would be difficult to resist the beauty of the calla, 'Schwarzwalder' (of the Black Forest). Although not particularly tall at 50cm (20in), it is one of the most dramatically and luxuriously black plants, with the rim of its black spathe tinged with deep carmine. It is certainly a more neighbourly alternative to my first choice for this scheme, the malodorous and rather phallic *Dracunculus vulgaris*.

Red has to be the colour of contrast for this devilish design, and it appears in the form of a small 40cm (16in) astilbe (also known as goat's beard), whose softly pyramidal blooms complement the upright spikes of the much larger black false hellebore; the latter dominates the back of the feature, with its large ribbed leaves above which 120–150cm (4–5ft) tall, deep browny purple-to-red spikes of flowers which will attract insects like multi-pronged forks of 'the Lord of the Flies'. Red also appears in the groundcover to the fore, with low-growing 10cm (4in) red stonecrop and the red autumnal berries of the mottle-leafed cuckoo pint (also known as lords and ladies) at 20–25cm (8–10in) tall. Both should be left to spread and naturalize in front of the hostas and euphorbia. The euphorbia, which can grow up to 75cm (30in), was selected for its dark purple leaves and green bracts which are also tinged with red.

But to lighten up this dark scene, I have used hints of white. White appears on the variegated leaves of the fairly large *Hosta fortunei* 'Francee' at 90 x 90cm (3 x 3ft) and, more boldly, on the smaller and slower-growing variety 'White Christmas', which reaches a 30cm high by 60cm wide (1x2ft) spread in five years. Solomon's seal, with its small pendulous white blooms and variegated leaves, adds movement. A more silvery splash of white is created by the use of the 15cm (6in) tall deadnettle, *Lamium maculatum* 'White Nancy' for additional ground cover alongside the red stonecrop and cuckoo pint. In fact the white/green-leafed theme continues with the cuckoo pint and the calla on waxy lush leaves which are sparsely spattered with white.

1. Black false hellebore, *Veratrum nigrum*
2. Bat plant, *Tacca chantrieri*
3. Solomon's seal, *Polygonatum odoratum* var. *plurifolium* 'Variegatum'
4. Astilbe
5. *Hosta fortunei* 'Francee'
6. *Euphorbia amygdaloides* 'Rubra' syn. 'Purpurea'
7. Calla, *Zantedeschia* 'Schwarzwalder'
8. *Hosta venusta* 'White Christmas'
9. Red stonecrop, *Sedum spurium* 'Schorbusser Blut'
10. Cuckoo pint or lords and ladies, *Arum italicum marmoratum*
11. Deadnettle, *Lamium maculatum* 'White Nancy'

GLOSSARY

N.B. Text words picked out in bold are included in the glossary.

ACIDIC SOIL
With a **pH** value of less than 7.0 denoting lime-free soil.

ALKALINE SOIL
With a **pH** value of more than 7.0. The greater amount of lime in the soil the greater its alkalinity.

ANNUAL
A plant that grows, flowers and sets seed in the same year, and then dies (e.g. the cornflower).

BASAL STEM
Shoot from neck or **crown** of plant.

BEDDING PLANT
An annual, bulb or **tender perennial** used for temporary display in borders, window boxes etc, that is replaced/discarded after flowering (e.g. the pansy).

BIENNIAL
A plant that completes its growing cycle in two seasons, i.e. does not flower in the first year (e.g. the hollyhock).

BRACT
A modified leaf at the base of a flower or flower cluster (e.g. on the euphorbia).

BUDDING
A method of propagation, usually for roses and ornamental trees, where a single bud of a named **variety** is inserted into the stem of a **rootstock**, and bound in with raffia or plastic tape.

BULBIL
A very small bulb that is usually found in the leaf axil (the joint between a leaf stalk and the parent stem) (e.g. on the lily).

CALYX
Collective name for **sepals**.

COLD FRAME
Garden equipment with sides of wood, plastic or brick and removable transparent top of glass or synthetic material.

COLD STRATIFICATION
(see STRATIFICATION)

CORM
A bulb-like organ created from a short, thickened stem covered with papery or fibrous **scales** (e.g. on the gladiolus).

CROSS-POLLINATION
The transfer, by insect or wind, of pollen from one flower to another on a different plant.

CROWN
Part of the plant at, or just below, soil level, from which new growth appears each spring (e.g. on the iris).

CULM
The jointed, hollow stem of bamboo and some ornamental grasses.

CULTIVAR
An abbreviation of 'cultivated **variety**', the term of classificition which denotes a member of a **species** that has been bred by human hand to differ in colour and/or size from other members of the same species. See also 'The Naming of Plants' (page ix).

DEADHEAD
To remove faded (spent) flowers or flowerheads regularly, to encourage a longer flowering period.

DECIDUOUS
A tree or shrub that sheds all leaves annually at the end of the growing season (e.g. the beech).

DIVISION
Splitting a plant during **dormancy** into a number of pieces, each with some root and shoots, for propagation or to maintain vigour in older plants.

DORMANCY/DORMANT PERIOD
The period when a plant is 'sleeping', i.e. between the end of one growing season and the start of the next.

EPIPHYTE/ EPIPHYTIC
A plant, such as moss and most orchids, that grows on another, but is not parasitic, instead obtaining nutrients from the air.

EVERGREEN
A tree or shrub that retains leaves throughout the year, while continually shedding and replacing leaves. See also SEMI-EVERGREEN.

FALLS
The downward falling petals of an iris. See also STANDARDS.

FAMILY
A classification term for the principal category of plant above **genus**. The name of a family of plants is often derived from that of the type genus (e.g. rosa (genus) Rosaceae (family)).

FLORET
A single flower in a head of many flowers.

FLORIFEROUS
Bearing or capable of bearing many flowers.

FULLY HARDY (see HARDY)

GENUS
A classification term for a group of related plant **species** that share similar distinctive characteristics. See also under 'The Naming of Plants' (page ix).

GERMINATION
When seeds or spores sprout, or form new tissue.

GRAFTING
A method of propagation, where the shoot of one plant is artificially joined with the **rootstock** of another.

GROUND COVER
Low-growing plants and shrubs that spread well, and are often effective at suppressing weeds.

HALF-HARDY
A plant unlikely to survive spring or autumn frosts. Usually raised from seed **under glass**, and planted out at the end of May.

HARDEN OFF
To accustom a cultivated young plant to outdoor conditions through repeated and gradually increased exposure.

HARDWOOD CUTTING
A cutting – usually about 30cm (12in) in length – that is taken from the mature shoots of trees or shrubs and inserted into open ground in late autumn to root.

HARDY
A plant able to survive outdoors throughout the winter.

HEEL CUTTING/ HEELED SOFTWOOD CUTTING
A cutting that has been deliberately cut to retain a small strip of bark or outer fibrous material from the main shoot. This heel often increases the cutting's chance of rooting successfully.

HERBACEOUS
A non-woody plant that dies back to the **rootstock** at the end of the growing season.

HORTICULTURAL FLEECE
A porous, fibrous 'blanket' that covers seeds and young plants to protect them from adverse weather conditions and some airborne insects.

HUMUS
Partially decomposed organic matter in the soil that improves the fertility and water retention of the soil and is therefore important for plant growth.

HYBRID
A classification term for a plant produced by the breeding of two or more genetically dissimilar parents. See also the section 'The Naming of Plants' (page ix).

HYBRIDIZER
A plant which easily produces its own hybrids (e.g. the aquilegia).

LAYER/ LAYERING
A method of propagation whereby a stem is encouraged to take root, by being pegged down into the soil, while still attached to its parent plant.

MARGINAL
Shallow water or moist soil around pool edges and banks of streams. Also used to describe plants suited to such a situation.

MULCH
Bulky organic matter (e.g. bark chippings, garden compost, leaf mould, manure) applied around the base of plants to conserve moisture and protect the roots from frost. It also reduces the growth of weeds and enriches the soil.

NECTARY
A glandular structure in the flowers and leaves of a plant which secretes nectar, a sugary fluid collected by bees and other insects.

NEUTRAL SOIL
With a **pH** value of exactly 7.0.

NODE
A joint on the stem of a plant from which leaves or lateral branches grow. When used in a cutting it has the ability to produce roots.

OFFSET
A short runner that arises naturally and produces roots and shoots at the tip to form a new plant.

OVERWINTER
To dig up tender plants, that are unable to survive winter conditions, and bring them indoors (or to bring in potted plants for the same reason).

PASTE
The white-coloured ring, of various widths, that runs around the centre of an auricula flower.

PERENNIAL
A plant that continues its growth for at least three seasons.

pH
A scale from 0.0 to 14.0 describing the degree of acidity of a substance (for example soil).

PILOSE
Covered with fine hairs.

PINCH OUT
To remove the growing tip of a plant to encourage side shoots for bushier growth or more flower buds. Also know as 'stopping'.

POTAGER
A small kitchen garden combining vegetables and decorative plants.

POT BOUND
Where a plant's root system has become too densely packed into too small a pot, causing the plant to deteriorate due to a lack of nutrients.

POT ON
To transfer to a larger pot to avoid the above condition.

POT UP
To transfer from seedling trays to pots.

PROPAGATION
The cultivation of plants by cuttings, layering, grafting, etc.

RACEME
An elongated, unbranched flowerhead consisting of several flowers (e.g. the kennedia).

RHIZOME
A thick, creeping horizontal underground stem with buds that develop into new plants (e.g. in iris and mint).

ROOTSTOCK
1. The **crown** of a plant plus roots.
2. The host plant which provides stem and root for **budding**.

RUNNER
A horizontal above-ground stem that roots at its **nodes** to form new plants. Sometimes confused with **stolon**.

RUST
A fungal disease organism with spores that appear as orange-red, yellow or white powdery blotches. Infected plant material should be burnt or discarded; never add to the compost heap, or the problem will be perpetuated.

SCALE
A specialized epidermal cell on the exterior of some **corms** and bulbs which can be used in **propagation**.

SEMI-EVERGREEN
A tree or shrub that retains leaves throughout the year in mild climates, while continually shedding and replacing leaves.

SEMI-RIPE CUTTING
A cutting from the same season's growth, that has stems which are becoming firmer (but not woody) and is just beginning to develop buds. The procedure is similar to that described for a **softwood cutting**.

SEPAL
The outer part of a flower that protects the developing bud. See also CALYX.

SOFTWOOD CUTTING
A cutting from a young and vigorous non-flowering shoot. The quickest type to root, but the most prone to rot. Use **stem cutting** or **stem tip cutting** method.

SOIL-LESS COMPOST
Bark, coir, sand or peat (if you must) mixes.

SPADIX
A fleshy flower spike bearing tiny stemless flowers (e.g. in the arum).

SPATHE
A modified leaf or bract that sheaths and protects the flower (e.g. in the arum).

SPECIES
A classification for a group of plants that are so closely related in terms of flower and fruit that they appear, superficially at least, to be identical. See also 'The Naming of Plants' (page ix).

STAKING
Using canes and hoops to support plants that have heavy flowers or weak stems. Supports can be invisible or decorative, according to taste.

STANDARDS
1 Plants that are trained to have a central unbranched stem.
2 The upright petals of an iris. See also FALLS.

STEM CUTTING
Cutting a length of stem into 5–10cm (2–4in) sections, each with a **node** at both ends, and removing lower leaves before dipping in hormone rooting powder and planting. Can be used for **softwood** and **semi-ripe cuttings**.

STEM-TIP CUTTING

A cutting taken in spring, where the stem is cut just below a **node** and the lower leaves removed. The stem is then dipped in hormone rooting powder before planting. Can be used for **softwood** and **semi-ripe cuttings**.

STOLON

A horizontal above-ground stem that roots at its tip to form a new plant. Sometimes confused with **runner**.

STOPPING (see PINCH OUT)

STRATIFICATION

A preparatory method for propagating certain seeds that need to experience one or more cold periods (but, in a few cases, a warm period of 20–25°C (78°F) to begin **germination**. Seed is stored in a free-draining medium, such as a sand/grit mixture, in a refrigerator (or heated tray). It is left for a specified number of weeks at a specified temperature, then sown.

SUCCULENT

A fleshy plant that has adapted to life under arid conditions by producing tissue in its leaves or stems to store water (e.g. the aeonium).

SUCKER

A shoot that arises from below ground level, directly from the root or rootstock of a mature plant.

TENDER PERENNIAL

A plant which is **perennial** in its native habitat, but which may only be perennial in harsher climes if grown in conservatory or greenhouse conditions.

THIN OUT

To discard weaker seedlings from a sowing (in seed trays or in situ), in order to allow adequate spacing for growth of stronger specimens. To 'prick out' means the same.

TILTHED

Ground that has been cultivated for growing plants.

TRIFOLIATE

Having three leaves or leaf-like parts, or three leaflets on a compound leaf.

TUBER

An underground storage organ derived from a thickened stem or root.

UMBEL

A flat-topped cluster of flowers, each flower's stalk rising from one central point (e.g. the cow parsley).

UNDER GLASS

Grown in greenhouse conditions.

VARIETY

A classification term for a member of a **species** that has naturally developed differences in colour and/or size from other members of the same species. See 'The Naming of Plants' section (on page ix), for further information.

BIBLIOGRAPHY

Baker, Margaret
Discovering the Folklore of Plants
Shire Publications, Tring, 1969

Beckett, Kenneth A.
The Royal Horticultural Society
Encyclopaedia of House Plants
Simon & Schuster, London, 1995

Boase, T. S. R.
Death in the Middle Ages. Mortality,
Judgement and Remembrance
Thames and Hudson, London, 1972

Booth, Michael Haworth
The Moutan or Tree Peony
Constable, London, 1963

Calloway, Nicholas (Editor)
Georgia O'Keeffe. One Hundred Flowers
Phaidon, London, 1990

Case Jr, Frederick W. and Case, Roberta B.
Trilliums
Timber Press, Portland, 1997

Clark, David
Pelargoniums. Kew Gardening Guides
Royal Botanic Gardens, Kew &
Collingridge, 1988

Clebsch, Betsy
A Book of Salvias. Sages for every Garden
Timber Press, Portland, 1997

Ellacombe MA, Rev. Henry N.
Plant Lore and Garden Craft of
Shakespeare
William Pollard, Exeter, 1878

Harding, Alice
The Book of the Peony
Waterstone & Co. Ltd, London, 1917
(reprinted 1985)

Hardy Plant Society, The
Look Who's in Our Garden
Pershore, 1998

Hepper, F. Nigel
Pharaoh's Flowers. The Botanical
Treasures of Tutankhamun
HMSO (Royal Botanical Gardens, Kew),
London, 1990

Hollander, Anne
Seeing through Clothes
University of California Press, Berkeley,
1975

Hyatt, Brenda
Auriculas. Their Care and Cultivation
Cassell Publishers, London, 1989.

Lamb, Edgar and Lamb, Brian
Pocket Encyclopaedia of Cacti in Colour,
including other Succulents
Blandford Press, London, 1969

Llewellyn, Nigel
*The Art of Death. Visual Culture in the
English Death Ritual c. 1500 – c. 1800*
Reaktion Books, London, 1991.

**Lötschert, Wilhelm and Beese, Gerhard,
trans. Clive King**
Collins Guide to Tropical Plants
Collins, London, 1983

Malins, Professor John
The Pruner's Handbook
David & Charles, Newton Abbott, 1995
(revised)

Phillips, Roger and Rix, Martyn
Perennials, Volumes I and II
Pan Books, London, 1991

Pollock, Michael and Griffiths, Mark
*The Royal Horticultural Society Shorter
Dictionary of Gardening*
Macmillan, London, 1998

**Reader's Digest Encyclopaedia of Garden
Plants and Flowers**
London, 1993 (revised)

Royal Academy of Arts (Catalogue)
*The Great Japan Exhibition. Art of the Edo
Period, 1600–1868*
London, 1981

Royal Horticultural Society, The
*Gardeners' Encyclopedia of Plants and
Flowers*
Editor-in-chief: Christopher Brickell
Dorling Kindersley, London, 1990

Royal Horticultural Society, The
RHS Plant Finder 1999-2000
Dorling Kindersley, London, 1999

Todd, Pamela
*Flora's Gems. The Little Book of Tulips. A
Garden of Poetry, History, Lore and
Floriculture*
Brown & Company, London, 1994

Vertrees, J. D.
Japanese Maples
Timber Press, Portland, 1987 (second
edition)

Wood, Henry J.
*Pelargoniums. A Complete Guide to their
Cultivation*
Faber & Faber, London, 1966

ABOUT
THE AUTHOR

Freya Martin's career has included six years with the British Diplomatic Service which she joined at the age of 17, three of which were spent in Sri Lanka. She left the stresses and strains of her life there to study ancient history at King's College, University of London, gaining a PhD in 1996.

Freya moved out of London to settle in the Heart of England, spurred by fond memories of childhood summer holidays spent on her grandparents' farm in Shropshire. From those early days Freya's mother has been an invaluable source of knowledge and encouraged her in all things horticultural, especially during the writing of this, her first book.

ACKNOWLEDGEMENTS

The author and Publishers would like to thank the following for permission to use their copyright photographs:

A–Z Botanical Collection Ltd. Front cover: *Maranta leuconaria kerchovia*, second down, *Tulipa* 'Queen of Night', bottom left; pp. 4, 5, 7 (cutout), 12, 15, 17, 18, 24, 29, 32, 41, 42, 45, 47 (bottom right), 48 (and on front cover), 49 (bottom right), 52, 54, 55, 57, 73, 76, 77, 83, 85, 86, 89, 93, 94, 105, 106 (top left) and 110 (bottom left). Back cover: *Cimicifuga simplex* 'Brunette', top.

Anthony Bailey: p 51.
Bob Brown, Cotswold Garden Flowers Nursery: pp. 23 and 64.
McOnegal Botanical: p. 75.
Freya Martin: i, ii, 6, 7 (border), 36, 58, 66, 67, 68, 72, 90, 95 and 111.
Eric Sawford: pp. 21, 39, 110 (top right) 112, 116, 124 and 128.

Harry Smith Horticultural Photographic Collection. Front cover, anti-clockwise from top left: *Dahlia* 'Tally Ho', top left; *Beta vulgaris*, third down; *Ocimum basilicum* 'Purple Ruffles', bottom right; *Helianthus* 'Prado Red', centre. pp. vii, 1, 2, 3, 8, 9, 10, 11, 13, 14, 16, 19, 20, 26, 27, 28, 30, 31, 33, 35, 37, 40, 43, 44, 47 (top left), 49 (top left), 50, 53, 56, 59, 60, 61, 62, 63, 65, 71, 74, 78, 79, 80, 81, 82, 84, 87, 88, 91, 92, 96, 97, 98, 99, 101, 106 (bottom right), 107, 108, 109, 113, 120, 121, 125 and 132. Back cover: *Viola* 'Black Beauty', centre and *Ajuga reptans* 'Atropurpurea', bottom left.

The author would like to express her gratitude to the following for giving her permission to photograph their plants:

Kevin Belcher, Ashwood Nurseries, Kingswinford, West Midlands: pp. 58 and 90.
Bob Brown, Cotswold Garden Flowers Nursery, Offenham, Worcestershire: pp. i, ii, and 66.
Bridge End Nursery of Gretna Green, at the Amateur Gardening Spring Show 1999: p. 36.
Mrs Clare Throckmorton, Coughton Court, Alcester, Warwickshire: p. 68
Pershore and Hindlip College of Horticulture Garden Centre: pp. 6, 7 (border), 72 and 95.

The author also gratefully acknowledges the invaluable input of her editor, Gill Parris.

INDEX

Note: Page references given in **bold** type indicate the presence of a photograph.

DOLLS' HOUSES AND MINIATURES

Architecture for Dolls' Houses	Joyce Percival
A Beginners' Guide to the Dolls' House Hobby	Jean Nisbett
The Complete Dolls' House Book	Jean Nisbett
The Dolls' House 1/24 Scale: A Complete Introduction	Jean Nisbett
Dolls' House Accessories, Fixtures and Fittings	Andrea Barham
Dolls' House Bathrooms: Lots of Little Loos	Patricia King
Dolls' House Fireplaces and Stoves	Patricia King
Easy to Make Dolls' House Accessories	Andrea Barham
Heraldic Miniature Knights	Peter Greenhill
Make Your Own Dolls' House Furniture	Maurice Harper
Making Dolls' House Furniture	Patricia King
Making Georgian Dolls' Houses	Derek Rowbottom
Making Miniature Gardens	Freida Gray
Making Miniature Oriental Rugs & Carpets	Meik & Ian McNaughton
Making Period Dolls' House Accessories	Andrea Barham
Making 1/12 Scale Character Figures	James Carrington
Making Tudor Dolls' Houses	Derek Rowbottom
Making Victorian Dolls' House Furniture	Patricia King
Miniature Bobbin Lace	Roz Snowden
Miniature Embroidery for the Georgian Dolls' House	Pamela Warner
Miniature Embroidery for the Victorian Dolls' House	Pamela Warner
Miniature Needlepoint Carpets	Janet Granger
More Miniature Oriental Rugs & Carpets	Meik & Ian McNaughton
The Secrets of the Dolls' House Makers	Jean Nisbett

CRAFTS

American Patchwork Designs in Needlepoint	Melanie Tacon
A Beginners' Guide to Rubber Stamping	Brenda Hunt
Blackwork: A New Approach	Brenda Day
Celtic Cross Stitch Designs	Carol Phillipson
Celtic Knotwork Designs	Sheila Sturrock
Celtic Knotwork Handbook	Sheila Sturrock

Celtic Spirals and Other Designs	Sheila Sturrock
Collage from Seeds, Leaves and Flowers	Joan Carver
Complete Pyrography	Stephen Poole
Contemporary Smocking	Dorothea Hall
Creating Colour with Dylon	Dylon International
Creating Knitwear Designs	Pat Ashforth & Steve Plummer
Creative Doughcraft	Patricia Hughes
Creative Embroidery Techniques Using Colour Through Gold	Daphne J. Ashby & Jackie Woolsey
The Creative Quilter: Techniques and Projects	Pauline Brown
Cross Stitch Kitchen Projects	Janet Granger
Cross Stitch on Colour	Sheena Rogers
Decorative Beaded Purses	Enid Taylor
Designing and Making Cards	Glennis Gilruth
Embroidery Tips & Hints	Harold Hayes
Glass Painting	Emma Sedman
How to Arrange Flowers: A Japanese Approach to English Design	Taeko Marvelly
An Introduction to Crewel Embroidery	Mave Glenny
Making and Using Working Drawings for Realistic Model Animals	Basil F. Fordham
Making Character Bears	Valerie Tyler
Making Decorative Screens	Amanda Howes
Making Greetings Cards for Beginners	Pat Sutherland
Making Hand-Sewn Boxes: Techniques and Projects	Jackie Woolsey
Making Knitwear Fit	Pat Ashforth & Steve Plummer
Natural Ideas for Christmas: Fantastic Decorations to Make	Josie Cameron-Ashcroft & Carol Cox
Needlepoint: A Foundation Course	Sandra Hardy
Needlepoint 1/12 Scale: Design Collections for the Dolls' House	Felicity Price
Pyrography Designs	Norma Gregory
Pyrography Handbook (Practical Crafts)	Stephen Poole
Ribbons and Roses	Lee Lockheed
Rosewindows for Quilters	Angela Besley
Rubber Stamping with Other Crafts	Lynne Garner
Sponge Painting	Ann Rooney
Tassel Making for Beginners	Enid Taylor
Tatting Collage	Lindsay Rogers
Temari: A Traditional Japanese Embroidery Technique	Margaret Ludlow
Theatre Models in Paper and Card	Robert Burgess
Wool Embroidery and Design	Lee Lockheed

GARDENING

Auriculas for Everyone:

How to Grow and Show Perfect Plants — *Mary Robinson*

Bird Boxes and Feeders for the Garden — *Dave Mackenzie*

The Birdwatcher's Garden — *Hazel & Pamela Johnson*

Companions to Clematis:
Growing Clematis with Other Plants — *Marigold Badcock*

Creating Contrast with Dark Plants — *Freya Martin*

Gardening with Wild Plants — *Julian Slatcher*

Hardy Perennials: A Beginner's Guide — *Eric Sawford*

The Living Tropical Greenhouse:
Creating a Haven for Butterflies — *John & Maureen Tampion*

Orchids are Easy: Beginner's Guide
to their Care and Cultivation — *Tom Gilland*

Plants that Span the Seasons — *Roger Wilson*

VIDEOS

Drop-in and Pinstuffed Seats — *David James*

Stuffover Upholstery — *David James*

Elliptical Turning — *David Springett*

Woodturning Wizardry — *David Springett*

Turning Between Centres: The Basics — *Dennis White*

Turning Bowls — *Dennis White*

Boxes, Goblets and Screw Threads — *Dennis White*

Novelties and Projects — *Dennis White*

Classic Profiles — *Dennis White*

Twists and Advanced Turning — *Dennis White*

Sharpening the Professional Way — *Jim Kingshott*

Sharpening Turning & Carving Tools — *Jim Kingshott*

Bowl Turning — *John Jordan*

Hollow Turning — *John Jordan*

Woodturning: A Foundation Course — *Keith Rowley*

Carving a Figure: The Female Form — *Ray Gonzalez*

The Router: A Beginner's Guide — *Alan Goodsell*

The Scroll Saw: A Beginner's Guide — *John Burke*

MAGAZINES

WOODTURNING · WOODCARVING · FURNITURE & CABINETMAKING
THE DOLLS' HOUSE MAGAZINE · THE ROUTER · BUSINESSMATTERS
WATER GARDENING · EXOTIC GARDENING · GARDEN CALENDAR
OUTDOOR PHOTOGRAPHY · WOODWORKING

The above represents a selection of the titles currently published or scheduled to be published.
All are available direct from the Publishers or through bookshops, newsagents and specialist retailers.
To place an order, or to obtain a complete catalogue, contact:

GMC PUBLICATIONS

Castle Place, 166 High Street, Lewes, East Sussex BN7 1XU,
United Kingdom

Tel: 01273 488005   Fax: 01273 478606   E-mail: pubs@thegmcgroup.com

Orders by credit card are accepted